The Ult Guide to Letting Go of Negativity and Fear and Loving Life

What I Learned on My Journey From Hater to Appreciator

Ted A. Moreno, C.Ht.
Certified Hypnotherapist
Success Performance Coach
www.TedsTipsBlog.com

Table of Contents

Acknowledgements

No one does it alone. If I have any happiness or success in my life, it's because there are many that took the time to share their wisdom, learning and encouragement with me. Although too many to mention, I'd like to give special and heartfelt thanks to:

My wife Natalie, who has always supported me, loved me and been my biggest fan, even when it wasn't easy to do so.

Trinity and Roxanne, my daughters and teachers.

My parents, Ted and Carmelita Moreno, who taught me how to work hard and how to love.

My brothers Eddie, Frank, Daniel, David, Jude, and John, and my one and only sister Christy, for keeping me humble.

Josephine Johnson, my mother in law.

Dennis Johnson, my brother from another mother, for his studio recording wizardry.

Brian Hansen, Misael Figueroa, Mike Millar, Donald Murdock and Becky Byrkit, the best friends a guy could have.

My BNI Rosebowl group, especially the late Jim Locke of ResultWorx for setting me up in WordPress, and Skye Moorhead of Skye Moorhead Photography for contributing her unique and wonderful images to my blog.

Craig "No BS" Valine, this book would not have been written without his coaching, generosity, support, and marketing expertise.

Michele Guzy, C.Ht. for pointing me in the right direction.

June Davidson for being there when I needed someone to listen.

Paula Denney for her invaluable generosity and support.

Jerry Brandt for his jokes, generosity and support.

Landmark Education, where the possibility was created.

Those authors and teachers who have profoundly influenced my life: Eckhart Tolle, Dr. Wayne Dyer, Deepak Chopra, Tony Robbins, Richard Bach and Carlos Castaneda.

All my clients, and readers of Ted's Tips for Transformation: thank you for letting me walk the path with you.

What People Say About Ted

General Self Improvement

Ted Moreno is a gifted Hypnotherapist who lives up to the highest ethical standards of his profession. I have experienced Ted's innate ability to help others achieve control over their lives. He employs his gift with empathy, skill and a generous spirit to provide real help. I enthusiastically recommend Ted Moreno. ~R. Idels

Ted is a very professional and caring hypnotherapist. He demonstrates knowledge and expertise in his field and knows how to get to the root of an issue to produce quick positive results. I referred several people and all have spoken highly of him. I would highly recommend Ted to help you overcome any issues that you may want to transform and change. ~J. Singer

I wanted to see for myself how Ted worked and went to him twice for hypnotherapy. I have to admit that I was skeptical, but after just one visit my life changed. Ted was 100% professional during our sessions and afterwards I walked out of his office feeling completely balanced. I have recommended him to several friends and will continue to recommend him because I believe in him fully. ~K. Erickson

Ted, you are truly gifted at what you do. This stuff is life changing for me, it's the best thing I've done for myself for a while! Thanks again. ~J. Lau

I received your CD a couple of weeks ago, I have listened to it twice this week and I LOVE it!!!! Thank you very much, it is wonderful!!! I will really enjoy listening to it. Friday will be the 90-day mark of my early morning walking regimen. That is truly a significant accomplishment for me, and I have you to thank for it! After many years of struggling to get a plan of self improvement in place, I now feel that it has happened. I have some great tools to work with and I have a partner in the journey....YOU!! ~Chris F.

Booking a series with Ted is like adding a few more tools to my tool box. My most recent series of visits helped me get focused on the right path again. Thanks Ted for your techniques that work! My goal is now identified and easily within my reach. Blessings! ~P. Scott

Most of my life has been spent in self-hatred, fear, and sadness. Ted has helped me see beyond what I have always known. Ted is an excellent hypnotherapist and has also been a great teacher and mentor in helping me face my fears. I have grown so much from our work together.

Thank you Ted for helping me see that the possibility of living a free and peaceful life does exist. I can see that it is right in front of me. All I need to do is declare it powerfully. Thank you Ted for always believing in me. ~L.H.

Ted makes you feel very comfortable with the process of hypnotherapy, and he takes the time to really understand the areas his clients should focus on. I had a wonderful experience with Ted, and would recommend him to anyone looking to open up new possibilities in their life! ~Kelley H.

Smoking

Dear Ted, it's been almost four years since I quit smoking. There's never been a "white-knuckle" moment, and I almost never even think of lighting up. On the extremely rare occasion that I do think about it, all I need to do is take a deep breath of fresh air without coughing, and the thought goes away!
The good part is, whenever I see anyone smoking these days, I still think to myself, poor schmuck, why are you doing this to yourself, don't you know how easy it is to quit!!! Thanks again. ~B. Freiberger

Just wanted to let you know, today is 6 months, no smoking, no trying to smoke, no holding a cigarette, cigar, pipe, etc. I feel real good. I am running three times a week and my long run is on Saturdays. I ran 12.5 miles this Saturday, non-stop. I have been adding every week and will stop this weekend at a 13 mile run. Thanks a Billion. ~Jim D.

Thank you Ted for your assistance helping me quit smoking. You saved my life. I also want to thank you for your positive suggestions concerning the 3 1/2 hour dental procedure that coincided with my sessions with you. You told me everything was going to go smoothly and that my recovery would be quick and successful. Indeed all of the above was achieved with a calm peace of mind. Once again, thank you Ted, you're the greatest. ~Dominic S.

Ted, I used your tape and the process you taught me to successfully quit smoking for my alcohol control. It has been over two weeks since I had a glass of wine or anything. *~Barb B.*

Dear Ted, Thank you so much for your help in giving me the tools to quit smoking- like most I have quit hundreds of times, but with your program I believe I will always be a permanent non-smoker. I tried hypnosis before for this and was not successful, your professionalism was very different than my previous experience, your knowledge of the struggles associated with quitting was obvious on the first visit- I followed your program as you laid it out and it made it much easier than expected. Again, thank you so much, and continued success on your mission to empower individuals like myself to succeed in life. *~J.P. Yarmolovich*

Anxiety

A friend and I took advantage of a 2 for 1 admission to the Glen Ivy Hot Springs and while there went into The Grotto (underground caves). Prior to going in I asked about the size of the place and explained my claustrophobia. They said there were emergency exits if I panicked so we went in. There were a few times when I felt I might give in and run out but did the thumb/finger rubbing and silently repeated the mantra "I'm okay in any surroundings"...and was able to enjoy the underground experience! I also went into the steam room and whereas I'll usually sit right by the door just in case; this time I went to the back of the room and was able to stay and enjoy the steam. You have definitely helped me.

Your comments, questions, and homework have helped me immensely. I was on the elevator about a week ago and a few others got on as well. I spoke w/them, smiled and stayed away from negative thoughts ... even when I thought maybe it had gotten stuck between floors (momentary lapse which I quickly pushed away) and then the door opened and I walked out smiling and proud that I'd remembered your advice. Again, thank you for how much you've helped me. *~R. Yáñez*

Ted, thanks for helping me enjoy driving. Even when a wrong turn happens, I recover without fear; it has been so freeing. But more than that, you've given me tools for my stated problems that have helped me in so many other areas. What you do is not a cure, but does help a person find a way to a better place within so the outside world is a much easier place to be. ~RB

Dear Ted, my life is changing because of the hypnosis sessions we have had. I feel confident in the tools you have provided to help me understand and control my fear and anxiety. It has given me the opportunity to look at situations in life differently with a quieter, calmer spirit. ~Jeannie

Dear Ted, I can't thank you enough! After nearly twenty years of anxiety and panic attacks, I thought my world was destined to remain "small". You helped me see that there is life without anxiety. Thank you. ~Tina

Performance Anxiety

I came to Ted when I wanted help dealing with my performance anxiety. I ride Hunter/Jumper horses competitively and I would become so nervous at horse shows, and even sometimes in practice, that my mind would race, and I would start to rush my horse, make mistakes or even go off course ... all of which does not win ribbons! After only a couple of sessions, I was definitely more relaxed and confident while I was riding! It was then that Ted made me realize that I should set my goals higher. Maybe my horse and I could not only place, but we could win! And win we did, our very next show we were Champion in our division. Eight sessions later, my riding has completely changed for the better, but more importantly, my life has changed. I am much more confident and I have a great positive attitude in every aspect of my life. I have learned that I have the power to achieve greatness in anything that I want, and that is a wonderful gift. Thank you Ted, I am looking forward to the journey." ~Donna C.

Fear of Flying

Thanks so much for your help. I had a few moments of panic up in the air, but made it through using some of your tips. But, I still made it!!! I'm even thinking of flying to San Jose for our next vacation--in about a month. It's not as far and I think I can do it. I even felt some of the same excitement I used to feel when I was younger--part of that was I'm sure your therapy. Thanks again! ~TRI

Test Taking

Ted is a professional dedicated to his craft and who consistently drives himself to a next level of learning to better help his clients by teaching, coaching and guiding with his knowledge and insight. Ted has perception and amazing patience, whether he is helping someone determined to quit smoking, or guiding someone else away from anxiety which doesn't allow them to comfortably enjoy a flight or relax when anticipating an uncomfortable situation.

Ted can be of amazing assistance to someone who has a difficult time preparing for tests. He provides tools for absorbing information and for releasing the anxiety which holds a person back from going through the door which will allow them to take and pass the exam. Thank you for the opportunity to put down some words in recommendation of Ted's services.
~*Armida Baylon*

Public Speaking

(The talk) went very well even though it truly was extemporaneous. Several people came up to me after and, as you use in your talk to me, shook my hand and congratulated me on what they said was a very good talk. I do feel my work with you had some positive effect. Thanks. ~*K. Kortchmar*

Business Success

I was very skeptical about hypnotherapy. Since I was trying to take my business to the next level quickly, I decided to give it a try despite my skepticism. After my first session with Ted, I quickly became a believer! Ted takes his work seriously and is truly gifted. Since I started seeing Ted, my business has started growing much more quickly. I am attracting and retaining the type of people who will be integral to the long term success of my business. I attribute much of the growth to a change in my mindset, which was brought about by my work with Ted! I would recommend hypnotherapy with Ted to anyone looking to make a change in their life or business. ~*M. Jackson*

Life Changes

It's been crazy, overwhelming and confusing since I left California. I don't think I would have been capable to have made such a smooth transition, if I hadn't had the chance to work with you. Thank you for sharing your wisdom, truthfulness and time with me. I will forever be deeply grateful. *~J. Lopez*

IBS (Irritable Bowel Syndrome)

Dear Ted, I just wanted to thank you again for all you have done for me. Removing the "cloud" of IBS from my life has lifted my spirits and enabled me to enjoy life. *~Karen W.*

Health and Wellness

I have used Ted personally, as well as, referred Ted to friends and family. He is an expert hypnotherapist and did wonders for my mother when she was ill. If you want results from hypnotherapy, Ted is definitely your guy!   *~J. Locke*

Relationships

The trip back to North Carolina over the holidays to visit with my parents went very well. Despite a few days at my parents' dealing with a snowstorm and subsequent power outage, it was relatively stress-free. When my mother would bring up topics that I did not wish to discuss, I would immediately tell her that we would not be having that conversation, and the topics were quickly dropped. The hypnosis session clearly helped, and I felt the nudge to move away from the old "parent-child" pattern of behavior that invariably would cause an argument. I greatly appreciate your help and am looking forward to working with you on future challenges. *~Jason B.*

Weight

I had the pleasure of working with Ted a few years ago to fundamentally change my internal thinking and subsequent behaviors around eating. As a person who has struggled for a lifetime with weight, I felt it time to work on the change from within. Ted is a masterful hypnotherapist and Certified Therapeutic Image Facilitator. Not only did I reach my desired weight, I have been able to maintain the weight level for several years now. I feel as if a fundamental change in my behavior has finally occurred.

Through a series of sessions that helped me create memory cues for myself, I often reach back mentally to regain the connections I established with the help of Ted. His work will always be a part of my life. Ted is a highly dedicated professional, with the utmost integrity. He is warm and personable and will assist you in a comfortable and relaxing setting. I highly recommend Ted Moreno as a helpmate in the attainment of your goals. *~Kathy Van Tassell*

Insomnia

Thank you so much for the hypnosis CD for insomnia. I played it last night, no TV either last night. I don't think I went through the whole CD, I was asleep. Ted your voice is a gift, it is so soothing to me. I woke up once last night but right back to sleep until 7am this morning; I usually wake up at 4 or 4:30am every morn. THANK YOU AGAIN TED! *~DS*

Introduction

I grew up as a cynical kid who complained a lot. Nothing was ever quite right. Although I was an excellent student in grade school and in my first couple of years of high school, by my senior year I felt bored with life. Nothing out there in the "real" world looked good enough to strive for.

After a couple of years of college in the Los Angeles area where I grew up, I left to attend the University of Arizona in Tucson in 1981. For the next five and a half years before I dropped out, I drifted aimlessly through college, partying, half-heartedly attending classes, and looking for some meaning to attach to my life. I wouldn't say that I was hateful, but there was not much that I really liked.

I clearly remember sitting on the steps of the dorm of a girl I was dating. She was smart, good looking and ambitious. I asked her what she wanted out of life. She said she wanted to give back to society. "Screw society!" I said spitefully. She looked at me, shaking her head, and said "You poor man, I feel sorry for you..." Needless to say, we didn't last too long.

After dropping out of school, I went from job to job, and relationship to relationship. Somewhere along the line I decided that I had no desire to ever commit to anything that would tie me down such as buying a home, getting married, having kids, or starting a business. All I wanted to do was hike, play hacky sack and party. I always rented the cheapest and smallest places I could find so I wouldn't have to work too hard. I was adrift on a sea of resignation and apathy, challenged by low self esteem and a lack of motivation and direction.

In 1990, a romantic relationship I was in fell apart in a matter of days. The resulting pain and sense of devastation took me by surprise, as we had only dated a few months. I was compelled to ask myself "What the hell is wrong with me?"

That event was the impetus that started me on my own personal journey of self development. I started reading books, doing yoga, meditating, and taking personal development seminars. I started to work on my self esteem. It began to occur to me that perhaps there was some value in a life of contribution and that I might even have something to contribute.

Nevertheless, by 1999, at 39 years of age, I was still living in a studio bachelor pad. I was working for a software company collecting credit card info over the phone from people that needed tech support for their software. I was making okay money but very unhappy; people have a tendency to scream at you when they think your software is buggy but you want to charge them for tech support. I was going through the breakup of yet another relationship.

The good side, if any, was that I was now taking a good hard look at myself, and I didn't like what I saw. After many years of blaming parents, employers, girlfriends, circumstances and society, it had become clear to me that the problem was me. At the same time, and more importantly, I started to develop compassion for the struggle of humanity to find peace, purpose, and meaning.

After much agonizing, I decided to leave Tucson and the beautiful Sonoran Desert, a place I had grown to love, to move back to Los Angeles, something I had sworn never to do. I just felt that I had to shake things up.

I moved back to Los Angeles in February of 2000. I started working for a friend (a decision that would end our friendship) at a non-profit organization. In October I met my wife to be.

In 2003, I was still working for my friend and miserable once again in a job I hated. I was at my wit's end. I had a sense that I wanted to help people as a therapist, but getting licensed as a Marriage and Family Therapist would take at least another 8 years. Then fate intervened.

Some co-workers and I were sent to attend a seminar on the topic of communication at a nearby hotel. The seminar leader was one of the best speakers I had ever heard. She also mentioned that she was a hypnotherapist. At a break I approached her to inquire about her training. She said that she had attended Hypnosis Motivation Institute in Tarzana and encouraged me to check it out. I will forever be grateful to her for those encouraging words.

I started training as a hypnotherapist in March of 2003. In October I got married. I graduated from hypnotherapy school in March of 2004 and started my hypnotherapy practice. I had my first child in 2005, and my second in 2007. By April of 2009, when my wife and I purchased our first home, I had done all the things that I swore I would never do. I guess I really did shake things up, didn't I?

❖

In April 2009 in the middle of the process of purchasing my first home, I decided to start writing a blog. I wasn't sure even what a blog was, or why I should write one, but the conventional wisdom of the time was that you should have one.

I set up a Word Press site and started writing about my life experiences, what I've learned, and a little about hypnosis and hypnotherapy. I called these blog posts *"Ted's Tips for Transformation"*. I found that I enjoyed writing, and soon, people were telling me that they were enjoying my blog posts, which made writing them even more fun.

As of the writing of this, I have posted a blog post almost every week since my first one in April of 2009. I find the act of writing to be quite fulfilling, often excruciating, at times painful, and always challenging. The most satisfaction I get, however, is when I reach deep down inside to write honestly and authentically about what I have discovered to be real and true during my short time walking this planet, and my readers are moved to respond.

This book consists of blog posts written between April 2009 and December 2010. I've edited the content from the original posts for clarity as well as to conform to the style of a book.

Most of what is contained in this book was written in my home office in San Dimas, (what my wife calls my "man cave"), usually on Saturday or Sunday mornings long before the rest of the world has risen for the day. In that space, and in the process of sharing my thoughts with others, I have come to a greater appreciation of my life, all that I have been blessed with, and my place in this strange and wonderful journey called life.

Ted A. Moreno

March, 2011

Part 1: Hypnosis 101

What is Hypnosis?

THEORY OF THE MIND

"How Hypnosis and Suggestibility Works"

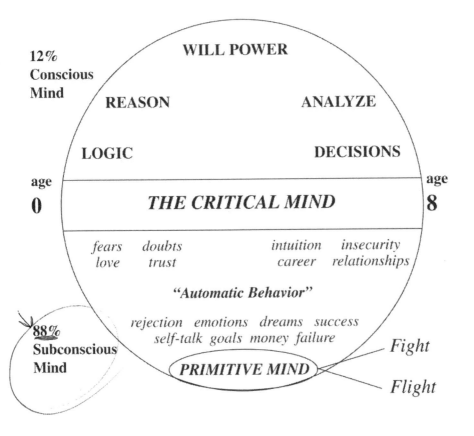

12%
Conscious
Mind

WILL POWER

REASON   ANALYZE

LOGIC   DECISIONS

age **0**   *THE CRITICAL MIND*   age **8**

fears doubts   *intuition insecurity*
love trust   *career relationships*

"Automatic Behavior"

rejection emotions dreams success
self-talk goals money failure

88%
Subconscious
Mind

PRIMITIVE MIND

Fight

Flight

Right Brain Suggestibility: The Emotional and creative side that listens literally but speaks inferred.
Left Brain Suggestibility: The logical and detail side listens inferentially but speaks literally.

My main tool for helping people is hypnosis. So exactly what is hypnosis? How does it feel? How is it created?

Hypnosis is a natural state we all go into. Let's go further into this.

As children, we believe everything we are told; we do not have the ability to analyze incoming information. We are said to be very suggestible. We actually learn how to be human. We learn likes and dislikes what we are capable of, what we are not capable of, what is fearful, desirable, etc. This is the creation of our so called Life Script: a collection of beliefs and "knowns" that shape our behavior and thinking. This happens at the level of our **subconscious mind**, we are not aware that it is occurring.

Somewhere between 7 and 9 years old, we start to develop an inhibitory process, called the **critical mind.** This blocks suggestions from going into the subconscious. We began to question incoming information, we began to ask why, and to seek to understand the information presented to us. At this point we begin to develop our **conscious mind**, which we use for decision making, reasoning, analyzing, and logic.

As you can see from the diagram above, the subconscious mind makes up 88% of our total "mind power" according to some estimates. The conscious mind, only about 12%. **The subconscious mind has a much greater influence on our behavior.**

Throughout our day, there is much information coming into our minds. Let's call this information "message units". These message units come from our environment, our bodies, our conscious minds (thoughts), as well as our subconscious minds.

Remember my story of me standing in front of a stack of boxes, having just moved into my new home, overwhelmed with the idea of unpacking? That's how hypnosis is created: an overload of message units, causing the critical mind to fail, allowing a state of hyper suggestibility, where we lose the ability to critically analyze incoming information.

Time to take a break! Wouldn't want to get overwhelmed...

How Hypnotherapy Can Help You Change

"There's a part of me that wants to change but there's another part of me that doesn't, and that part always seems to win out!"

Sound familiar? There is a lot of truth to this statement. What we are talking about is a conflict between *two minds*: the conscious mind and the subconscious mind.

To put it in plain English: the reason it is so difficult for folks to change is because the subconscious mind makes up 88% of your mind, and it likes what is known and familiar. It does not like to change. Your conscious mind makes up 12% of your mind and oftentimes cannot overcome the power and influence that the subconscious mind has over our behavior and thinking. To make changes in our lives, we must get our subconscious mind on board so that it starts to become familiar with the change we want to make. Hypnotherapy is a very effective way to do this.

Here's an illustration of how this works. Let's say you are born into a family where both your parents smoke. As children, we believe everything we hear and see. You hear dad saying all the time "I need a smoke". Dad seems pretty happy after he has a smoke. So does mom. One day you ask for a cigarette. You are told cigarettes are for "big people". You want to be a big person too. As you grow up, the people that care for you, love you, and keep you alive, smoke. This becomes your reality. Grownups smoke and they seem to really like it.

A few years down the road, you are smoking too. Maybe you started smoking to fit in with other kids who smoke. Perhaps life got a little challenging and somehow you knew that smoking would make you feel better about these challenges (think adolescence). Maybe you were bored one day, came across your parent's cigarettes, and stuck one in your mouth. Soon, you are acting out a "script" given to you in childhood which goes like this: to be the person you want to be (cool, tough, grownup, etc.) you must smoke.

Fast forward to 2009. No one seems to like smokers anymore. It's getting darn near impossible to find a place to smoke. Cigarettes are outrageously expensive. And just last year, your mom was diagnosed with emphysema. You start thinking about quitting. You try a few of times to quit but it lasts only a couple of days. That time you quit for three days you almost strangled the kid behind the counter at Starbucks because the foam wasn't right in your latte. You try gum and decide that that really sucks. The patch helps a little but it's just not the same as pulling that pack out, smacking it against the palm of your hand, pulling out a cigarette with your mouth and lighting it with your favorite lighter. Man! That first hit. You may wonder how you can ever quit; it's all you've ever known! It's who you are, it's what you do, it's what you like, why, cigarettes are almost your.....*friends.*

But deep down inside you are starting to suspect that these may be false friends. And that these "friends" may be killing you, at least that's what everyone says. Maybe you try again to quit, half heartedly. You start to become resigned that you may never quit. Then someone tells you that they quit with hypnotherapy. You look up a hypnotherapist, give him call, and make an appointment. You wonder what's going to happen.

What happens of course is that you come into my office and quit in one session. Let me explain how hypnotherapy works using the example of smoking cessation.

How Hypnosis Can Help Someone Quit Smoking

To repeat, the reason it is hard to change a habit such as smoking is because your subconscious mind (which makes up 88% of your mind), likes what is known and familiar and sees change as unpleasant or painful. The conscious part of your mind which makes the decision to quit, (12% of your mind) can't compete with the strong influence of the subconscious mind. The physically addictive part of smoking plays a part as well; however, after about three days, this usually passes. It is the mind which makes it difficult to quit.

When working with a smoker, the first question I ask over the phone even before they come into my office is *"Why do you want to quit?"* I'll start getting them focused on freeing themselves from smoking and why that is important. My smoking cessation program involves four weekly sessions. They will quit at either the first or second session. At the beginning of each session, I will ask them "Give me the reasons why you want to free yourself from smoking." I'll have them write their reasons down on a 3x5 card and carry it with them. Repetition and reinforcement is the key to affecting the subconscious mind.

For the first 30-40 minutes of each session, we'll talk about when they smoke, why they smoke, what triggers them to smoke, and provide techniques for helping them deal with urges after they have quit.

The last 20 minutes of the hour session is the hypnosis part. Remember, during hypnosis the subconscious mind is much more open to suggestions. What we will do is create familiarity in the mind of the smoker to how good it will feel as a non smoker. We'll do that partly with visualization; imagining a healthier life without smoking. I'll give their reasons back to them in hypnosis. I'll help them create a strong belief that not only is it possible for them to quit, but that quit they will.

With enough repetition and reinforcement of new ideas and habits of thinking and behaving through hypnosis, the subconscious mind begins to align itself with the conscious desire to quit. If the motivation is there, quitting happens so easily that many ex- smokers are quite surprised. No wonder that smoking cessation is the number one reason people go to a hypnotherapist.

Part 2: Ted's Tips for Transformation

"All hypnosis is self hypnosis"

Every Day Hypnosis or How to Put Yourself Into A Major Trance

Buy a house. That's how I did it. I walked into the garage of my new house stacked with *my life in boxes* and tried to decide where to start. Immediate overwhelm.

Don't get me wrong, I'm grateful that we can buy a house. Here's the point: **this is an example of how we go into trance pretty much on a daily basis.** Hypnosis is trance, and trance is a natural state we all experience. Ever miss your off ramp on the freeway? This is a classic example of environmental hypnosis; your eyes are fixed on a point in front of you, the drone of the motor lulling you, your mind far away thinking about something else. There are lots of other examples: getting so caught up in watching television that you don't even hear someone calling your name. (If you have kids you know what this looks like!) How about when you're listening to music that transports you to a different place? TRANCE.

I sometimes wear my hypnotherapist badge when I'm out and about trying to help the ailing economy by spending my hard earned money in a store or coffee shop. Oftentimes, the person behind the counter will say "Oh, you're a hypnotherapist; I'd better not look at you!" (I can't help but come back with a smarty pants answer like "You'd better not or I'll turn you into a toad.")

This is a common misperception many people have, that hypnosis is something *done* to you. In fact, *all* hypnosis is self hypnosis. When you come into my office for a hypnotherapy session, I will help you to achieve a state you have been in countless number of times. The difference is, it's under controlled conditions where positive suggestions are given to you that are in line with what you (the client) want. (You will not bark like a dog or cluck like a chicken unless that's what you want, and I do charge extra for working with animals.)

An example of a hypnotic state under uncontrolled conditions is watching the news on television. You become hypnotized by sitting still, fixing your gaze on the talking heads, and having a passive mental attitude. Television news is designed to provoke an emotion. Most of the time these emotions are fear, sadness or anger. You may have an inner commentary about these emotions such as "That's terrible!", "Oh my God, how sad.", "Boy that sucks!" or "I'd better watch out for that (virus, terrorist, murderer, economy, etc.)" Lately, the message from the news media has been loud and clear: "Be afraid, be very afraid!" **Think about how this affects your mental state.**

Another example of uncontrolled, environmental hypnosis: It's Monday morning in my new house after spending the weekend moving. There are boxes everywhere. I can't find my underwear. I'm tired. Which box do I start on? Then the inner dialogue starts: "This is going to take forever. I have no idea why this coffee doesn't seem to be working, is it decaf? Renting was easier. God, I have so much to do. Where the heck is my underwear??!!"

Fortunately, I am fairly present to when I am becoming overwhelmed. And here's what I do, and you've probably heard it before: **Sit down, close your eyes, take a few deep breaths, and say to yourself, "It's going to be OK, I can handle this, just take it one box (minute, hour, day etc.) at a time."**

"You will not bark like a dog or cluck like a chicken unless that's what you want!"

"You can tap into the quiet place inside of you."

Toads and Deep Relaxation

I was thinking about toads as I fell asleep the other night. Spadefoot toads to be exact. You might be thinking: what do toads have to do with deep relaxation? Well, it started with the weather.

Friday I woke up and it was raining. In June. In all my collective years here in the Los Angeles area (30 years), I have never seen rain in June. I was pleasantly surprised because I love rain. I lived in Tucson, Arizona for almost 20 years, and the best part of that experience was the summer rains that desert dwellers call monsoons. These are summer lightening storms; sometimes very dramatic, always welcome and refreshing at a time when everything alive and some things that aren't are withering from intense heat.

The rain brought back vivid memories of those summer rains in Tucson. As I lay in my bed that night, I imagined myself back in Arizona, on the front porch of some old house, watching the rain come down in sheets. I was told once that you never forget the smell of the Sonora Desert after it rains. I found this to be true that night as once again I smelled the wet creosote, and breathed in the thick moistness of the warm air. I thought about the song of the toads, awakened from their slumber by the gods of thunder.

At first, I felt an aching to be back there, but suddenly this was replaced by gratitude the likes of which I have not felt for quite some time. All the tension and stress of my life disappeared. Concern and worry about the circumstances of my life faded. I realized that I had been blessed with these experiences; they were mine to savor whenever I wanted to, they could not be taken away from me, and I felt supremely grateful. I found myself in my own *special place* as I fell into a peaceful sleep.

As a Certified Therapeutic Imagery Facilitator, *"Special Place"* is a tool that I use quite often in my practice with my clients. You can use it as well anytime you want, when you desire peace, comfort, ease, and relaxation.

Here's what to do: Simply sit or lie down, be still and take some deep breaths. Focusing and relaxing each part of the body can be helpful. (This is called a progressive relaxation). See if you can tap into the quiet place inside of you. Then imagine, pretend or visualize a place that you have either been to or have seen. Or, you can create one in your mind's eye, with the elements you desire. Make sure this is a place that represents relaxation, peace, tranquility, serenity. See if you can connect with the sights and colors, shadow and light. Notice if you are sitting, standing or lying down. Check if there are any scents or smells to this place. See if you can hear the sounds. Give yourself suggestions along the lines of "I am in my special place, and in this place I am safe and secure, happy and in control, peaceful and relaxed."

If you practice this a few times, soon you'll be able to quickly create a powerful image that can be used whenever you want to produce a very relaxed and comfortable state.

And if you should meet any spade foot toads in there, please say hello for me.

"You can use Special Place anytime you desire peace, comfort, ease, and relaxation."

"The number one thing you should do when you're down is to reach out to someone who cares."

The #1 Thing You Should Do When You're Down

I don't like to complain, especially about my health. I guess I'm kind of stoic in that area; I figure people have enough problems of their own, so unless they're a doctor, they really don't need to hear about my health. I must say that I'm fortunate; I'm a healthy fellow, and I really don't have many health issues.

However, I'm dealing with a health problem now that result in a significant decrease in my energy. In addition to that, my kids were generous enough to pass along the runny nose virus they picked up from day care. Suffice to say that I've been moody, irritable, and somewhat of a drag to be around. With the exception of my wife, I haven't really been interested in sharing that with anybody.

I come from a big family, 7 boys and 1 girl, including myself. I'm fortunate that we are all in close proximity here in the LA area, including my parents, so we are able to gather quite regularly at their house for food and drink. It had been a while since I'd seen my parents, and since they'd seen my two girls, their grandkids. In spite of my stuffy nose, lack of energy, and sour disposition, my wife and I chose to pack up the kids and drive out to East LA to visit the folks.

Sitting at the kitchen table with my parents, wife, and a couple of brothers, the conversation quickly turned to my haggard appearance and less-then-jovial demeanor. It didn't take much prodding for me to tell them about my health challenges. They were interested. They asked questions. Of course, they gleefully gave me grief as well; as is their nature *("He can't handle living with three women!!")* Later, three of my brothers and I packed into a car and went to get some food. When we got back, my sister-in-law asked me, "Why did all of you have to go to get the food?" I replied, "Because they're my brothers and I like being with them." She didn't believe me but it was the truth.

When it was time to leave, I said good bye to my father. He gave me a big hug (and he's not really a big hug kind of guy), put his hand on my forehead and said "Be healed, I hope you are feeling better." And I was. Much better.

The number 1 thing you should do when you're down, depressed, out of sorts, and really challenged by life, is to reach out to someone who cares. Give yourself permission to ask for help if you need it. Put aside your pride and call or visit a friend or family member. Let them know what's going on with you. Tell them how you are feeling. Sometimes, just talking to someone can be healing. If you don't feel you have someone in your life that cares, then contact a mental health professional, priest or minister, whoever you feel most comfortable with. If you are so inclined, go to church, temple or mosque and talk to whoever is your Deity. Write down your thoughts and feelings in a journal; get them out of your head and onto paper where they will be much less scary. Get a massage. Get out into nature, and let the trees, wind and water nurture your soul.

Nobody does it alone, so don't feel like you have to. It may sound corny, but we really do need each other. After all, we are all in the same boat, floating on a little blue ball though dark and empty space, trying to make the best of it. If you are alone and feeling isolated, and have been for some time, consider that perhaps that is what you've chosen, on some level. You can choose different. Of course, you will have to take responsibility for how you are feeling; it does no good to keep complaining to everyone unless you are willing to take some action. But perhaps reaching out would be the first step in doing that.

Letting someone know that you are not well does not mean you are weak, it just means that you are human.

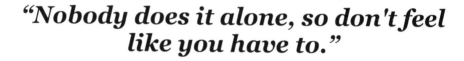

"Nobody does it alone, so don't feel like you have to."

"Identify the things you need to be doing daily to achieve your goal."

The Secret to Programming Your Mind For Goal Achievement

I'm going to reveal to you a secret that I have been using for many years to increase my motivation and to keep me on track to achieve my goals. This is but one example of the kind of tools I give to my clients to help them program their minds for success. Like I said, I use this myself and it really works.

It's very simple and involves affirmations. Now before you start going on about the Stuart Smalley character on Saturday Night Live, let me assure you that there are many ways to do affirmations and some are more effective than others.

First, pick a goal that you want to achieve and decide what the actions are that you need to be taking **now** to achieve the goal. For example, say you like to ride road bikes and you want to do your first century (100 miles) event. Of course, you need to be realistic. If you have not ridden more than 5 miles ever and the event is 30 days away, well, sorry but, it ain't gonna happen.

Next, identify the things you need to be doing daily to achieve your goal of riding in your first 100 mile ride in a time that gets you to the finish line before dark. To start, obviously, you need to be riding everyday or almost every day. What you want to do is to craft an affirmation that is specific and relevant. *"I'm riding my bike every day"* would not be as good as *"I am riding my bike at least 30 miles daily and at least 60 miles on the weekends."* Then, come up with two or three more that support your goal. How about *"I am eating the right foods that give me energy and stamina when I train."* or *I'm enjoying the feeling of getting stronger and more conditioned each time I ride."* You get the picture.

Next, write the affirmations down so that you have them exactly how you like them. Then, within half an hour before bed time and within half an hour of waking up, ***hand-write*** them once each. **It must be handwriting.** It doesn't matter how crappy your handwriting looks, printing is not near as effective. Now say the affirmation out loud while reading it so that you involve the sense of sight and hearing in addition to the physical (kinesthetic) process of writing them. Then picture in your mind, for just a few seconds, yourself doing the behavior you want to do.

Do the affirmations at night and in the morning for 30 days before you change them. Make sure you frame the affirmations in the positive as opposed to the negative. You don't want *"I am not sitting in front of the TV eating Cheetos when I should be training on my bike."* Start with *"I am..."* or *"I am becoming..."* or *"I have..."* etc.

Why handwriting? Why the half hour before bedtime?

Remember, we are all in hypnosis on a daily basis; half an hour after we wake up, and half an hour before we go to sleep. Our subconscious minds are suggestible at these times so why not give ourselves some positive suggestions? These are the magic 30 minutes to take control of your mind. This is when you want to read motivational or positive material. This is the time to read and say your affirmations. Your mind is open to suggestions at these times, be careful what you put into it!! The absolute last thing you want to do is to watch your local news before bed and hear about how many people were murdered or assaulted in your city. Make no mistake about it, this is often the leading story of the nightly news, and for good reason: to capture your attention and keep you watching. Read or listen to something that educates, motivates or inspires you instead.

Last week I talked about handwriting your affirmations. Handwriting is more of a right brain function, where as printing is more of a left brain function. We have a tendency to use our left brain function more often as this is the logical, linear side of the brain. However, it is the right side of the brain that is creative and intuitive. This is a generalization as both types of functions can span hemispheres. The point is that by handwriting it is possible to stimulate the creative part of our brain to find solutions to challenges that stand in the way of our success.

This exercise can be a powerful way to affect your mind program it for success. Try it for 30 days and see what happens, using the same affirmations each day. OK!!

"This exercise can be a powerful way to affect your mind program it for success."

"How much of the voice in your head is really your own?"

What about that Voice in Your Head?

Yes, you have a voice in your head.

You may be thinking: *"What voice? What is he talking about? I don't have a voice. Maybe he has a voice in his head, but I certainly do not have one in mine."* Well, that's what I'm talking about. It's OK; we all have a voice in our head. Maybe more than one.

There are many ways to describe this voice. The Ego, Monkey Mind, Internal Chatter, Running Commentary. It's how we make sense of our world. We judge, we analyze, we compare. We search for meaning, patterns, and relationships. What most people call this voice is Me. I. Myself.

Did you ever have the experience of saying something out loud, and then you thought to yourself *"That is totally something my (mother, father) would say."* Is that your voice? Or is it your mother or father's voice? (or grandmother, grandfather, teacher, coach, etc.) **How much of the voice in your head is really your own?**

There's the story of a woman that was entertaining some guests one evening; she decided to cook a roast. When she served the roast, the guests noticed the ends of the roast had been cut off. When asked why this was, the woman replied *"That is how my mother always did it; it makes the roast taste better."* A lively discussion ensued when one guest, having worked in a fine restaurant, insisted that cutting the ends off of a roast does nothing to improve the flavor. Finally, the woman decided to settle it once and for all. She picked up the phone and called her mother. *"Mom, why did you always cut off the ends of the roast?"* *"Well my dear"*, her mother replied, *"My oven was so small, a whole roast would not fit."*

Consider this: you don't need to believe everything you think.

In my hypnotherapy practice, I call it self talk. The question I ask my clients is: Is your self-talk serving you? Think about it: how do you talk to yourself? Do you call yourself names, even in jest? Have you ever had any of these head conversations?

- I am no good at _____
- I'm a failure
- I'll never be able to ____
- Nobody likes me
- Boy, am I stupid.
- I'm such an idiot.
- I hate looking at myself in the mirror.
- Nobody will go out with me because I'm too (old, young, dumb, unattractive, poor, shy, fat, skinny,etc.)

A very wise person once told me "There is no reality without language." If indeed that is true (not really sure myself, but the statement is intriguing) then we are truly creating our reality with our language, thought by thought, sentence by sentence. We end up believing the reality we create, and we act (behavior) from these beliefs.

So be careful of what your say to yourself. That is, be aware of how you talk to yourself. What is possible for yourself will be created in your language.

If your self-talk is not serving you, that is, if it is holding you back, limiting you, making you feel bad, sad, angry, confused etc., then you must change it. You can change it. It's **possible.**

"What is possible for yourself will be created in your language."

"Who am I, really?"

I Think, Therefore I (Really do Have A Freakin' Voice in My Head!)

In the last chapter I discussed the phenomenon of **the ongoing inner dialogue** commonly known as **"self talk"** that we all experience.

There are many aspects of this discussion, ranging from the deeply philosophical to the obvious and mundane. I'll keep it simple: On the one hand, there is the **concept of the ego** and the question of *"Who am I, really?"* one of the basic dilemmas of existence. On the other hand, there is for many people the awareness that there are habitual patterns of thinking that are at the very least **self- limiting**, if not **self-defeating**.

Descartes, the seventeenth century philosopher, is famous for the statement "I think therefore I am" (Cogito ergo sum), which he saw as a primary truth. Three hundred years later, another famous philosopher, **Jean Paul Sartre**, realized that when you are aware that you are thinking, that awareness is not part of thinking, something he felt Descartes had overlooked.

Try this on: let us assume for a second that who you are is not your thoughts. Consider that who you really are is the **thinker of your thoughts.** That is, who you are is the awareness that you are thinking or that you have a thought. Stay with me for a second here, OK? As I see it, the problem that plagues us as a species is that we really believe that who we are is our thoughts:

- I am no good at this...
- I am good at this...
- This is who I am...
- This is who I am not...

Who we think we are, we can call our *story*. Each of us has a story about who we are. For the most part, this story is not real, it's invented by us, or it is an invention that we inherited from our primary caretakers. Consider the two statements:

My business failed.

- I am a failure.

The first is a statement of fact, that is, what happened. The second is a story about what happened, an interpretation. We can agree that not everyone who has had a business fail on them considers themselves a failure.

I believe that one of the most important skills that we can learn to develop is to be able to make the distinction between what happens to us and the story we make up about what happens to us. To be understand that most (if not all) of our thoughts are stories (interpretations) of events, and may have little to do with what happened.

This is all about learning to be detached from the thought process so that you become able to observe your thoughts.

In many ways this is the essence of meditation, or mindfulness practice: to simply sit and observe the monkey mind in action. Journaling, or writing down your thoughts in a journal can be a very effective way to develop awareness of your thoughts as well. Of course, a psychotherapist or hypnotherapist can help you make the distinction between you and your thought process.

What is the benefit of being able to observe our thoughts and see that they are not who we are? Turn the page for the answer.

"Most of our thoughts are interpretations of events, and may have little to do with what happened."

"We believe the voice in our head and most of the time we do what it tells us to do."

Had Enough About The Voice In Your Head? (Don't Worry, It's Just The...Well, You Know)

By now you may be thinking, "What is this thing he has with the voice in the head? Can't he write about something else? Like how to make a bunch of money really quick?"

Don't worry, it's just the voice in your head talking, pay it no mind.

I closed the last chapter with the question: What is the benefit of being able to observe our thoughts and see that they are not who we are?

The short answer is: *because **we believe the voice in our head and most of the time we do what it tells us to do**.*

Once you have the ability to somewhat objectively be aware of your own thought process, then you can start to have an awareness of habitual patterns of thinking that are self-limiting, self defeating, or self destructive. As long as you believe that you **are** your thoughts (the voice) then you will identify with your thinking. It's possible to become so identified with one's beliefs and ideas that you may be willing to kill someone to defend what you believe to be true.

This is one reason why the history of our species is one of violence and bloodshed. It may be true that it's the nature of mankind to be violent. Nevertheless, because of our capacity to be aware of our thinking and hence, to change it, we *can* change our nature. As a species, we have yet to develop a deep and lasting connection with who we are beyond *who we think we are.* (**I'll** save my ideas about *who we are* for another chapter.)

Ask yourself this question: How much of what you **think** most of the time is no more than *programming?* Remember, it's not what **happens to you** that matters, it's what you **think about** what happens to you that will determine your course of action or inaction. What you think about what happens to you is your **interpretation or story**. This interpretation is in a large part determined by your past experiences, culture, upbringing, religious beliefs, education, and current peer group.

As a hypnotherapist I help my clients to be aware of and identify stories that they hold as *beliefs* that are holding them back from what they want to have, be, or do. I help them to see that since these stories are in a sense *inventions* that are maintained by the "voice", that they are free any time they want to invent a new story that is empowering, encouraging, and inspiring. I help them instill these new beliefs using the **power of suggestion through hypnosis.**

In closing, let me leave you with this: ultimately, whether what you think about yourself is true or not is irrelevant. What matters is: **what does your thinking do for you?** Move you forward or hold you back? Give you joy or despair? Help you to love or disconnect you from loving? Help you grow or keep you stuck? You have a choice in what to think and believe about **anything.**

"As a species, we have yet to develop a deep and lasting connection with who we are beyond who we think we are."

"Something is lost there, in time and age, but so much more is gained."

For Everything Lost, Something is Gained

I was checking out You Tube one evening, watching Joni Mitchell play *"A Case of You"*. A song of incredible sadness and vulnerability, it speaks of lost love and the pain of letting go. The raw honesty and the craftsmanship of the song's album, *"**Blue**"*, made it a commercial and critical success and helped establish Mitchell as one of the most influential singer-songwriters of the late 20th century.

I stayed up late into the night watching videos; from 1965, Joni Anderson, before she became Mitchell, on a Canadian hootenanny show, *Let's Sing Out*, in black and white, fresh faced, a young girl on the verge of realizing a dream.

In another, more recent video, a much older Mitchell in front of an orchestra singing *"Both Sides Now"*, her trademark falsetto gone now, and in its place, the smoky and husky voice of age and experience. I wondered how it felt for her to sing this song about perspective, 30 years after she penned it. Perhaps she felt more keenly the truth of her lyrics that *"something's lost but something's gained"*.

I continued wading into the video past of 70's singer-songwriters, (yes I am aging myself, that's kind of the point) I came across a live version of **James Taylor** and Mitchell singing a duet on Taylor's *"You Can Close Your Eyes"*.

A few more clicks and there's a video of one of James Taylors early television appearances; young, almost adolescent, a full head of hair, wispy moustache, looking like someone needs to give him a good meal. He sings *"There's a song that they sing when they take to the highway, a song that they sing when they take to the sea"*. His journey took him through self commitment to a mental institution and 18 years of heroin addiction. He talks about this in another video; he is balding, lines in his face, in the sunset of his career. *"I should have died four or five times"* he says.

Next, I'm watching videos of **Sting** and **Allison Krause** playing at a James Taylor tribute. **Would there have been a tribute if he had not experienced what he did?**

These are songs I grew up with, and they made me think about my own journey. Closing down my computer close to 1 a.m., I went outside to my backyard, stood in the full moon's glow and thought about my travels as a single guy.

I remembered playing my guitar alone in a cabin in Montana, in the shadow of the Continental Divide. I recalled partying and dancing joyfully with fellow members of a theater group, at the director's house in Bisbee, accompanied by whatever we could find, egg shakers, bongo drums, and claves. In my mind's eye I looked down from the top of Wasson Peak on solitary monsoon clouds drifting across the Tucson basin like air ships floating over a desert sea.

Other memories came to me as well, not as pleasant. Sitting in a Civil War battlefield in Petersburg, Virginia, miserably unhappy, wondering why the hell I was so far from home. During that time I came to understand why someone would want to kill them self. I thought of standing on the mall at the University of Arizona, watching the same moon, cold and alone.

I went inside my house and checked on my sleeping children, and lay down in bed next to my sleeping wife. I missed my carefree life, playing music, hiking, travelling. It's true that something is lost there, in time and age, *but so much more is gained*. Maybe more valuable than what you lost, if you can choose it to give it to yourself.

The song that you sing when you take to the highway is not the song you sing when you take to your plow. On the highway there is exploration, out in the fields that you work, decision. There's an intention there to create, to plant a seed, to stick around and nurture it and to see what you can harvest, even if you don't feel like doing it. Transformation can happen in an instant, I have seen it, but most of the time it is a slow process, sometimes painful, almost always messy, as we struggle out of the skin of what we are comfortable with and into what are becoming.

To move forward you must let go; it's not easy and sometimes it's not pretty. Change will happen with or without you, but transformation, that is, change into who you want to be, *that* requires intention, focus, energy, and a willingness to be comfortable with being uncomfortable. If you are lucky you can make it happen. If you are luckier it may happen to you.

Discography

"A Case of You" from the album *Blue* (1971) *by* Joni Mitchell, Reprise Records.

"Both Sides Now" from the album *Clouds* (1969) by Joni Mitchell, Reprise Records.

"You Can Close Your Eyes" from the album *Mud Slide Slim and the Blue Horizon* (1971) by James Taylor, Warner Bros. Records.

The lyric *"There's a song that they sing when they take to the highway, a song that they sing when they take to the sea"* is taken from the song "Sweet Baby James" from the album *"Sweet Baby James"* (1970) by James Taylor, Warner Bros. Records.

"... all peak performers in any field of endeavor have a coach."

Someone to Believe in You When You Can't

Instead of learning to be cool with the girls, I made the incredibly boneheaded move of joining the cross-country team my freshmen year in high school. I ran more miles in high school than most people walk in a lifetime, or at least that's what it felt like. Upon joining the team, I was told that the coach was the also the Spanish teacher. Like most nerdy fifteen year olds, I thought I knew everything, and I figured that he'd just make us jog for a couple of miles every day. Wrong.

This coach introduced me to a level of physical pain that I have not encountered since. We didn't jog a few miles every day; we trained by running until we didn't think we could run anymore. And then, we ran some more.

There was a park not far from my high school: La Loma Park (the name still gives me the shivers). Coach would say, "Let's jog to the ole' La Loma". We would jog the three miles from our school to the park, then we'd run a practice course the coach laid out.

The course started with a wickedly steep grade and continued half a mile in length through the hilly, undeveloped part of the park. Coach would say something like, "We're going to run this 3/4 speed (25% less than all-out), and we are going to do it 10 times." We would look at each other as if to say "Can he be serious??" Running it twice could cure you of running forever. I remember feeling resentful - "How could he ask that of us?" The next thought would be "Why am I even doing this??"

We would run that miserable course over and over until our legs felt like Silly Putty. Just before we were ready to fall to our knees and beg for mercy, the coach would say, "OK, I guess 8 times is enough. Let's go home."

Looking back, I don't know how I was able to do what the coach asked. I felt that he would ask for an effort that was not only unreasonable, but simply undoable. But do it we would; we never considered otherwise. We finished the season as the fourth best cross-country team in Southern California.

The reason: the coach asked of us what we **could not and would not ask of ourselves, and in delivering that, we moved beyond what we thought was possible.**

I walked away from that experience with a confidence in my physical capability that has never left me, and that has allowed me to hike to places that left me in awe and wonder. (Havasu Falls in the Grand Canyon comes to mind).

Consider that all peak performers in any field of endeavor have a coach that provides direction, accountability, support and motivation. Why not you?

As a Success Performance Coach, my personal development program can help you take your goals, dreams and desires to the next level. As your success coach, I'll be your partner in helping you

- *Discover what's important in your life; your values and dreams*
- *Identify your strengths, skills and resources for success*
- *Create goals that are in line with your values and dreams*
- *Design a plan for achieving those goals*
- *Eliminate obstacles or blocks that stand in your way*
- *Celebrate and enjoy your success*

Success Coaching is different from hypnotherapy in that there is no hypnosis. It can be done in person, or over the phone, and at a pace you feel comfortable with. This may be every week, bi-weekly or even monthly.

Fortunately, you don't need to experience pain or exhaustion to benefit from coaching. You just need to be a winner who wants more out of life.

I didn't really enjoy cross-country that much (I switched to the track team the remaining three years: shorter distance, more glory). I constantly thought about quitting. I didn't for one reason only: the coach, who believed we could go the distance when we couldn't.

"You've got to do is to immunize your mind to the virus of negativity."

How to Keep from Catching the Mind Flu

When I was 12 years old I read "War of the Worlds"* by HG Wells. The book was really scary and the image of giant alien tripods stayed with me for a long time. When I saw the most recent movie version though, something else stuck with me that I didn't remember from the book. (Beware: Movie Spoiler!) The aliens die in the end because they had *no immunity to the diversity of bacteria and viruses to which we developed immunity millions of years ago*. I thought that was cool; the aliens were killed off by the common cold. They probably weren't getting enough sleep, being busy destroying the world and all...

Since I've had kids I've been catching two or three colds a year. Sheesh! I'm too busy to be sick! Lately, though, since this whole H1N1 thing, I've been reading a lot on how to avoid getting sick.

The key to staying healthy is to have a strong immune system so that you can fight the cold and flu bugs that are always around us. For example, many health and wellness practitioners recommend keeping your immune system strong by getting enough sleep, avoiding sugar, taking the right supplements, and managing stress. They suggest that getting chiropractic adjustments, acupuncture or massage can be helpful as well.

Consider that your mind works the same way. Let me ask you, have you ever had the experience of catching what I call the **mind flu**? Perhaps one day you became aware that you'd become so negative, discouraged, and defeated that even your dog didn't want to hang out with you for fear of catching it. You caught the negativity bug! Like the famous motivational speaker Zig Ziglar says, you were infected with stinking thinking and needed a check up from the neck up!

What you've got to do is to **immunize your mind** to the **virus of negativity** that is always out there: in the news, on the internet, in social conversation, in your own language, in your mind.

So how do you keep your mental immune system strong enough to ward off the mind flu that always threatens us? By taking your **mind vitamins**! Supplement your mind daily with positive material that keeps your mental immunity strong. Always be listening to **motivational or inspirational** material. Exercise and expand your mind by reading literature that **challenges you and inspires you**. How about a "mental adjustment" or mind massage" by coming in for a **hypnotherapy session**? It's perfect for a quick reduction in stress.

Reading books by authors that motivate and inspire has essential in keeping me **inspired** to be **positive and focused** on my goals. My favorites are authors such as Wayne Dyer, Maxwell Maltz, Richard Bach, Tony Robbins, Og Mandino, Napoleon Hill and Eckhart Tolle. Reading material by these authors has really impacted my life and can help you keep your mind so healthy that no negativity bug can infect it.

As prevention or cure for the mind flu, these books have worked for me and still do. Remember, the negativity bug is everywhere! Stay strong by taking your mind vitamins every day.

* Wells, H.G. *War of the Worlds.* London: 1898, William Heinemann.

For more information about the authors mentioned:

Richard Bach: http://en.wikipedia.org/wiki/Richard_Bach

Wayne Dyer: http://www.drwaynedyer.com/

Napoleon Hill: http://www.naphill.org/

Maxwell Maltz: http://en.wikipedia.org/wiki/Maxwell_Maltz

Og Mandino: http://www.ogmandino.com/

Anthony Robbins: http://www.tonyrobbins.com/

Eckhart Tolle: http://www.eckharttolletv.com/tv/

"Supplement your mind daily with positive material that keeps your mental immunity strong."

"What are you ready for now that you weren't ready for previously?"

What Lies Dormant Within You?

When I was living in Arizona, I tried to make it a point to come to Los Angeles every year at the holidays to see my family for three or four days. I'd stay at my parent's house; the house in which I grew up.

During the day, both my folks would be at work and since the other birds (my siblings) had long since flown the coop, there was just me hanging out.

I'm a person who enjoys solitude, so I always looked forward to that time. I would walk from room to room in my parents' house, looking at framed photos, thinking about all the time that had passed since I had left to be on my own. I'd think about my childhood, and people I'd lost touch with. Sometimes I'd read, or play my guitar, or just sit and think in the quiet stillness.

One day I went out to the backyard to walk around and noticed one of the trees had completely lost all its leaves. All that remained were sticks. It looked dead. I remembered that the last time I had visited LA, in spring, it was big and full and had flowers on it. I wondered, "What's keeping it alive?" What was going in on there? It occurred to me that maybe the tree was like me, just kind of hanging out and being quiet for a while. A crazy thought occurred to me that maybe the tree was reflecting on its life, in anticipation of the burst of energy that is Spring, in the revolving cycle of the seasons.

December 21st is the shortest day of the year, the winter Solstice. There's that sense of dormancy, quiet, shutting down for a while. I think it serves us to take a cue from nature and do the same.

I invite and encourage you to take some quiet time to reflect over the past year and get in touch with what is possible for you in the future. Focus on the good stuff that happened to you. Get a journal or some paper. Ask yourself some questions about the past year and write down the answers:

- What challenges did you overcome?
- What challenges stopped you?

- What did you accomplish?
- What remains left undone?
- What did you learn?
- What potential became real in your life?
- Who have you become that you were not one year ago?

I think there's great value in doing this. You can become present to your own self-development and growth.

But I think the most important question to ask yourself during this introspective time of year is this:

What lies dormant within me that is ready to awake?

See yourself as part of the cycle of the seasons. We all get our leaves stripped off of us at times. Sometimes we feel that we will be taken down by the winds of circumstance and change. But we can come back with renewed energy and life. It's in our nature. **Be at peace now with what happened over the past year. It's done, it's over. Take the seeds of growth that were given to you, take the lessons, the wisdom and the learning, plant them in your mind and move forward.**

Get really clear about what you want for your life. Maybe you are unsure, but as motivational speaker Les Brown* suggests, tell yourself "It's possible!" Everybody talks about taking massive action. For now, do some massive dreaming! Consider that what you thought wasn't possible for you in the past is no longer valid because you are not that person anymore. You have a whole year of new experiences, wisdom and learning.

What are you ready for now that you weren't ready for previously? How are you stronger and more prepared to take something on, to be more engaged with life, to play a bigger, more confident game? I guarantee you that there is something: writing a book, learning an instrument, learning a language, stepping into a new relationship or recreating an existing one, a new job, greater health, prosperity, happiness. **Discover it.** You may have to dig a little in some cold and frozen soil but it's there. It's waiting, and the world is waiting for you.

*For info about Les Brown, go to www.LesBrown.com

"Take some quiet time to reflect over the past year and get in touch with what is now possible for you in the future."

"The key to living a successful life is to decide what you want and go after it."

The Key to Success Is...

Before I tell you what I think the key to success is, let me tell you a story.

My wife and I were shopping for a house in early 2009. We had been looking for more than a couple of years. At times it was a grueling experience. Most times we had to do this after work, dragging our two small daughters along, all of us tired and hungry. The mix of tired and hungry kids with nothing to do and tired and hungry parents trying to talk to a realtor can be a lethal combination.

We looked at condos. We looked at houses with 1 bedroom and 1 bath and we looked at 2 bedrooms, 2 baths. We looked at houses with big yards, little yards and no yard, garage/no garage, we looked at everything but couldn't find something we liked. It was very discouraging at times.

Most of the time I was highly resistant to the whole process. Although buying a house seemed like a good idea, it seemed to be almost not worth the hassle. My wife, God bless her, did most of the work, dealing with listings, realtors, appointments and paperwork.

By early 2009, the economy had gone to hell, and home prices had hit bottom. We stopped looking at condos and started focusing on single family homes. We looked at more houses: some with big yards, some with no yards, garage, and no garage. It was then that we decided that a yard was important for our kids and that a garage was necessary for storage.

To make a long story short, we continued to make decisions about what we were looking for. Eventually, *we became clear about what we wanted: a two bedroom, two bath house with a yard and detached garage, and possibly a spare bedroom/office for the only guy in the family to go hide out in when the female energy got too intense.* We submitted some offers. At this point, I made the decision to let go of my resistance to the process of home buying, and focus instead on the outcome: having our own home.

I believe it was in late February that we walked into a house built in 1946 that had two bedrooms, two baths, a large yard, a detached garage, as well as a bonus room that could be used as an office. We are living in that house today.

The moral of the story? The more **clear** we became about what we **wanted** in a house, the easier the process got and the quicker we moved towards getting what we wanted.

I believe that the key to success is knowing what you want.

Sounds simple, doesn't it? Yet, I would say that very few people really know what they want. They are pulled this way and that way by the desire of the moment. They let their focus get pulled away from what they want by the multitude of distractions that our modern life offers. **The key to living a successful life is to decide what you want and go after it.**

What is success? I think the best definition I've heard comes from Paul J. Meyer* who said: *Success is the progressive realization of personal, predetermined, worthwhile goals.* According to this definition, if you know what you want, and are taking steps to get it, then you are a success.

Notice we are talking about the *key* to success. Knowing what you want is the key because it opens the door. But that's only part of the process. The other part is you **must take action by walking through the door.** In other words, when you decide what you want, you won't waste time on doors, or paths that don't lead you where you want to go. The Latin root of the word decide means to "cut away." This implies that you cut away various other distractions, alternatives, and temporary desires, leaving you to focus on one thing only: what it is that you want.

Spend some time thinking about what it is that you want. Write your thoughts down on paper or use a journal. I've been using a flip chart and a whiteboard which is really helpful since I tend to be visual.

In the following chapters, we'll talk about the power of goals in helping you get what you want. For now, remember that accomplishment starts with deciding what it is that you want. That's the first step.

*For info about Paul J. Meyer go to www.PaulJMeyer.com

"Accomplishment starts with deciding what it is that you want."

"If your goals are not written down, they are no more than wishes."

Opening the Door to Success: GOALS (Guarantee Overcoming Anything Limiting Success)

My four-year old daughter who I call The Chick asked me the other day when she could ride her new tricycle. "Tomorrow" I replied. "But Dad" she exclaimed, "Tomorrow's a long time!"

If only that were still true. If you're like most people, the things you were going to do tomorrow keep piling up as quick as the days pass. You've heard it before: "I was going to do it but life got in the way."

That's why only 44% of Americans bother to make New Year's Resolutions. The rest have decided they don't work. Like like banging your head against the wall, it accomplishes nothing except to give you a headache. In fact, instead of making resolutions, it might just be better to bang your head against the wall and save your self-esteem the beating you might give it when you find that your resolutions have fallen by the wayside.

If you made some New Year's resolutions, good for you. However, if you want to make any lasting change, there's a strategy for doing it and "resolving" to change is not it. I suggest that we throw out New Year's resolutions (if you haven't already) and institute "New Year's Goals."

In the last chapter I revealed what I believe is the key to success: **knowing what you want.** That's the first step, the key that opens the door.

The next step is where 90% of people stumble. **You must take your thought or resolution about what you want and turn it into a goal.** What's the difference?

First of all, you must write down your goal. If it's not written down it is just a wish. Sometimes wishing upon a star can make dreams come true but I wouldn't count on it; they have a better chance if you write them down as a goal (sorry, Jiminy Cricket.)

Get yourself a notebook or journal and write down what you want to have, do, or who you want to be. If you are serious about this goal, then it becomes a project, something you attend to daily, (kind of like having a kid). Dedicate a notebook or journal to this project.

Now, you may have a number of things that you **want.** The key here is to ask yourself, "What am I willing to **commit to as a goal**?" Focus on goals that will have the most impact on your life and that you feel you can reasonably get started on now. Some of your goals may not be fully formed or that you think you'd like to do but are not fully committed. Put those in a "later" or "back-burner" category.

Now you have three or four goals that you can focus on and commit to right away. **You may have heard of the SMART formula for goals.** What you want to do now is to set your goals using the SMART formula: *Specific, Measurable, Attainable, Realistic, Timetable.*

- *Specific. What exactly do you want to accomplish? Be very clear*. Describe it exactly. "In 2010, I am doubling last year's income" is a lot better than "I want more money." As Tony Robbins would say to that, "Here's a dollar, get outta here!" Make sure you state them positively, for example, don't say, "I don't want to feel strapped financially anymore"
- *Measurable. How will you know when it's achieved?* How will you track your progress? If a goal is measurable, then the results you want will be clear in your mind.
- *Attainable. You must believe that it is possible for you to get what you want.* Develop a written plan for achieving your goal so that you have a roadmap that confirms in your mind that there is a way to get what you want. Also, identify roadblocks and obstacles that may come up and how you can overcome them.
- *Realistic. Be honest with yourself.* Is it really something you want, or something you think you should have? Is this goal realistic for what is going on in your life? Is it consistent with your values? If not, then it's not realistic.
- *Timetable. When will you have it?* Put some urgency on it by assigning a deadline. Many folks don't like deadlines. Why? Because it puts pressure on them to perform.

That's exactly the reason you want deadlines. Deadlines act on you, affecting your body chemistry to react to the timetable you've set.

They prepare your body, your mind and your attitudes to respond effectively. They create a challenge and help support a positive attitude. Don't underestimate the power of a timetable.

That's what you've got to do to guarantee the highest chance of success for your goals. Sounds like work? You betcha. Do it anyway, I know you're up for it.

"Make the decision to be the person you need to be to get what you want."

Who Do You Have To Be To Get What You Want?

In the last chapter we discussed **how to create goals.** You take a desire, you turn it into a goal by writing it down using the SMART formula, and you make a plan. That's what you do. However, there is another very **another important part to getting what you want.**

In 2003 when I signed on the dotted line to register for **hypnotherapy school**, a very familiar and habitual thought came into my mind. It went something like this: *"Are you really going to do this? You've started a lot of things that you have never finished. Are you really going to use this education?"*

I have to admit, that was a very scary voice. At that time in my life, I was desperate to find a meaningful and enjoyable career to which I could apply my passion, enthusiasm, time and energy. Becoming a hypnotherapist seemed like what I had been looking for. But the voice was right; I'd had many jobs, started many things that kind of petered out. The idea of going to school, investing time and money, and wasting it all by not following through, well, frankly, it horrified me.

At one point the voice started up with "If this doesn't work out, maybe you can try..." Suddenly, in my mind I said **"Stop!** *This is it. I will make it work out. I will not let this opportunity pass me by without giving it my best shot. I refuse to consider that this won't work for me."*

What I had done was to make a declaration: I was no longer a person that started things and didn't finish. To get what I wanted, I needed to become a person who followed through. The first thing I did was to book a hypnotherapy appointment for myself to make sure that I continued to become that person.

Maybe you've had an experience like that. Where **who you were changed because of a decision you made.** Let me suggest that it really is that simple. **You must make the decision to be the person you need to be to get what you want.**

It may be uncomfortable, it may be unfamiliar, and you may not know what it looks like. But your personality will have to change. I have heard people say, "I'd like to have that (goal) but I'm not that kind of person that can do that, it's not in my nature...." Bullpoop! **You can change your nature.** To go from where you are to where you want to be, you must.

Here are some qualities that I believe are essential for anyone that sets goals and intends to achieve them.

You must be a person who is goal oriented. You must believe that it's important to have goals and to work to achieve them. If you are not willing to become one of these people then stop reading this right now, get yourself some Cheetos and go watch television. You must be a person who desires to accomplish something. You must be a person who sets goals regularly. It all starts there.

You must be a person who is comfortable with being uncomfortable. What you are doing now is comfortable. If you are not getting what you want, you must do something different. Doing something different will feel uncomfortable. Be OK with that. Realize that there is no change without discomfort. Expect it, and step right into it.

You must become a person that learns to overcome inertia and takes action now. Inertia is the tendency for bodies to remain at rest. This can be applied to minds as well. It's hard to get off the sofa to go out and jog. But once you are jogging, it's a lot easier to continue to put on foot in front of the other. That's because once you start, you have momentum that carries you forward. Inertia affects us all. To get what you want, you must learn to overcome it and take action. Period.

You must be courageous. It can be scary to set a goal. It's risky. You must have the courage to take risks. What if you fail? What if you don't do it right? What if there are obstacles? Rest assured, there will be obstacles, and you can count on it. Be courageous and start anyway and deal with the obstacles when they come. You might be afraid to face your own weaknesses. You're not good with people, money, sales, travelling, speaking in public, etc, etc, etc. You can learn. Having courage doesn't mean you are not afraid, it means that you move forward in spite of the fear, and everyone has fear. Even you. Yes, you.

You must be supremely confident. I almost typed "You must *have* confidence." But confidence is not something you have, it's something you are. You say you are not confident? **You can become confident.** You can learn.

Taking the steps I outlined in the last post to create your goals will give you confidence. Confidence simply means you have developed the belief that you can and will accomplish your goals.

You must be determined. By determined I mean you refuse to be stopped, side tracked, or distracted. Have you heard the story of how Sylvester Stallone sold his script for the movie "Rocky"? It truly is one of the most inspiring stories I have ever heard and a testament to dogged determination. You can find it on You Tube as told by self help author Tony Robbins*.

You must be a person who can generate energy and motivation. There will be days when you will not feel motivated. Sometimes you will not have the energy. If there is something you need to accomplish, the absolute worst thing you can do is say is "I don't really feel motivated" or "I don't have the energy". Say *"Even though I don't have the motivation or energy, I'm going to do it anyway."* Let's face it folks, lack of motivation is one thing and one thing only: a bad habit. Lack of energy can be the same thing although there may be dietary or other physical issues that may need to be addressed. If you really want to achieve your goals, you will address them.

The good news is, you don't have to do it all on your own. Take a self-development course or seminar. Call a therapist or hypnotherapist (preferably me). Read a book. The human mind is one of the most powerful forces on earth. What are you doing with it?

Go to www.youtube.com and type in the search box "Tony Robbins Tells Rocky Story."

"Self-care is vitally important and necessary to leading a happy and fulfilling life."

How Selfish are You? (Part 1)

You would not believe the bad luck I've had lately. I can hardly believe it myself.

One night last week I was watching television. It got later and later but I just kept watching it, even though I knew I should go to bed. I watched TV until 5:30 am, and then I slept for an hour and a half. When my daughter The Chick tried to wake me I snarled at her and she started crying. Boy was I tired and grumpy!

Since I woke up late I didn't get to eat breakfast before work. By the time I was done with my first client I was starving! There was some Halloween candy in the lobby of my building so I ate a bunch of candy corn, Tootsie Rolls and mini Three Musketeers. If I thought I felt bad before, I had another thing coming - I developed a horrible stomach ache! Can you believe that!?

During my session with my next client, she actually got up and said, "I'm leaving because you keep falling asleep while I'm talking to you. And why don't you wipe that chocolate off of your chin?" What nerve! Can you believe the bad luck?

It seemed as if I was doomed to have a wretched day so I cancelled the rest of my appointments and went home determined to force myself to work like a dog on computer stuff that's been piling up. I worked all afternoon. My wife came home with the kids but I kept on working. She said that dinner was ready but I kept on working. She said that dinner's done would I help clean the kitchen but I kept on working. She asked if I would help put the kids to bed but I just had too much to do! Then she got really angry with me and we had a big fight. Can you believe the rotten luck I had that day?

If you know me, then by now you may have guessed that none of that really happened (I don't like candy corn.) But if it was true you might be saying "You didn't have bad luck, you were just being irresponsible!" And that would be true.

In the imaginary scenario I just described, it can be summed up like this: I was not being responsible for my own self care. Taken to that extreme, I would say that I was being negligent; neglecting my own basic needs, therefore, I ended up neglecting the needs of those I love.

I've come to the conclusion that self-care is vitally important and necessary to leading a happy and fulfilling life.

How is your basic self-care? Are you getting enough sleep? Eating right? Taking care of your health? If you are neglecting any one of these, chances are that you are seeing the consequences in some part of your life.

But let me suggest that self-care doesn't end there. There is another level: Are you learning? Growing? Spiritually, mentally, emotionally? Are you having fun, experiencing joy, and giving yourself opportunities to become the best you can be? Paying attention to your loved ones?

The great business philosopher Jim Rohn* said "The greatest gift you can give to somebody is your own personal development. I used to say, 'If you will take care of me, I will take care of you.' Now I say, 'I will take care of me for you if you will take care of you for me.'"

For many, the idea of being good to yourself or taking care of yourself flies in the face of everything we have been taught about being selfish. "Don't think about yourself, think about others. Help others. Care for others. Don't be selfish by focusing or thinking too much about yourself.

We are all selfish on a most basic level. Everything we do we do, we do because we get something out of it. This is one of our drives as human beings. I'm not advocating living your life totally for your own pleasure and amusement, I'm suggesting that living your life for everyone else may leave you wasted, burned out, resentful, and no good to anyone, least of all you! After all, you're no good to your child on an airplane if you are passed out because you put their oxygen mask on first. You've got to take care of yourself first.

Much of life is about balance. And the hard cold truth is that it's not easy to do. In fact, for some of us, it may be easier to live for everybody else because it gives us an excuse to shirk responsibility for ourselves and our needs, especially if that was your model growing up. If that is the case, it can be really hard to do something else. However, you can unlearn what you have learned and honor your needs and wants so that you can give more fully give to others. You can't give away what you don't have!

To learn more about Jim Rohn, go to http://www.JimRohn.com

"We are all basically selfish."

How Selfish Are You? (Part II)

Something has come to my attention lately that I find quite astonishing and frankly, disturbing.

In fact, I'm not even sure how to write about this because it cuts pretty close to the bone for most people.

What is astounding to me is the number of people I come across, not just in my practice but in the outside world, **who don't honor themselves**. Either that or they just plain *don't like themselves*. They can't hold themselves in high esteem.

Now, they don't usually come out and say "I don't like myself", or "I'm not worthy", but it is apparent by their actions.

They don't eat when they need to. They don't get enough rest. They don't do things for themselves. They don't take care of their health. They don't engage in activities that fill them up, instead of engaging in activities that are depleting. They have insane schedules. They refuse to reach out to others when they are troubled. They don't give themselves credit. They tear themselves down. It's almost an epidemic, at least in our culture.

Now, I'm not immune to this epidemic. I'm feeling a little run down these days, a little wasted. I haven't been getting enough sleep, eating right, or getting enough exercise. Other things in my life seem to be higher on the list of priorities. I think I like myself and I think most people would say the same about themselves. Yet, I still don't care for myself the way I know I should.

It seems to me that many people take better care of their cars than they do themselves. And I think it's safe to say that most people take better care of others than they do themselves. Why is that?

Because we've been taught that it's bad to be selfish.

Let's be clear about one thing, and you don't need to be a psychologist, anthropologist or sociologist to see the truth of this: **we are all**

basically selfish. It's the human condition. Everything we do, we do in an attempt to satisfy some kind of physical, emotional or spiritual need. The question is, can we be ok with that fact?

Now, please understand, I'm not advocating that you forego all the kind and generous things you do for others to focus only on your needs.

If you have something extremely valuable, let's say for instance, a pet, then you will go out of your way to care for it. Why? Because you realize it's worth in your life and how it adds to your enjoyment of life. You feed it, bathe it, take it to the vet, give it love, and make sure it's happy. For Pete's sake, you even clean up its poop!

Here's what I think is the crux of the problem: **most of us simply don't realize our own value.** And if we have some idea of our own value, we have a tendency not to honor it. Why are you valuable? In my opinion, it's because you were born. I think that because of that fact, you have something to offer here in this life, and life is waiting for your contribution, or maybe already benefitting from it.

Is that true? Well, let me suggest that whether it's true or not doesn't matter. It's simply a really good place to stand. Stand in the place of **"I am valuable and have something to offer and I should take the best care of myself that I possibly can so I can do what I came here to do."** It's the declaration of your own value and self-worth that will help you to do the things that a person of value will do.

If you are valuable, then you deserve the best of care. You have something to offer your family, as well as your community, both local and global, and you must be up to offering your unique contribution. And to be up for that you need to be at your best, giving yourself what you need so that you can give to others.

The first thing you should give to yourself is **acceptance.** Tell yourself **"I'm ok. In spite of all the areas of my life where I perceive I fall short, I'm ok and doing the best that I can."**

Being valuable, being worthy, and being ok don't come from what you are doing.

If you base your value and worthiness on what you are doing than you run the risk that what you are doing will never be good enough.

Being valuable, worthy, and ok comes from saying that you are and believing it, then looking for areas in your life that support what you say. You will find them.

Let's throw out the word selfish. How about Self Caring? Are you willing to be self care-ful? Full of care about yourself?

Take care of yourself. We need you around. You have important work to do that only you can do. You may not feel that what you are doing is important but you don't know what life is preparing you to do. Accept the fact that you are human and will make mistakes. Be your own best friend. Be kind to yourself in word, thought and deed. Accept yourself for who you are and who you are not. Don't worry about doing it perfect. As the Buddha said on his deathbed, "Do your best".

"Why are we so afraid to ask for what we want and what we need?"

Go Ahead and Ask, I Dare You

A Job, a Yacht, and a Very Expensive Car

In 1987 I had a sales job that involved going into people's homes and trying to sell them stuff. It was a very tough gig. It was the kind of deal where the managers of the business wore flashy jewelry, drove flashy cars and yelled a lot.

I decided that I wanted a Porsche. Now, at this point in my life I was barely able to make my $250 rent, and this sales job was not helping. But I had read some books about goal achievement, so I cut out a picture of a Porsche and hung it on my wall. I even knew enough to write it down, and it went something like this: *"I'm driving a Porsche down I-10 listening to a Dire Straits cassette."* (One of my favorite bands at the time). Now, please keep in mind that I was in my 20's, single, naïve, and a little bit of a knucklehead.

Somehow, a few months later, I managed to win a sales contest during a period of "feast" in my sales (as opposed to famine). The prize was that the winners would get flown from Phoenix, Arizona, where I lived, to Huntington Beach, where the owner of the company lived. We would sail with him on his yacht to Catalina Island where we would have a nice dinner then spend the night in a motel. Which we did. The next day, on the yacht while sailing back to the mainland, the owner of the company and I were talking.

"So Ted," he asked me "What kind of car do you see yourself driving?"

I have no idea why he asked me that question as opposed to "What are your goals?" or "What do you want out of life?", but I definitely had an answer. "I would like to drive a Porsche!"

So he made me a deal. If I agreed to open a franchise in Tucson in the next few months, he would put me in a Porsche today. "Sure!" I replied, of course. He got on his boat phone and made a short call. "What color?" he asked. "Red" I said.

When we arrived at Huntington Harbor, there, sitting on the dock, was a brand new, 1987 Porsche 930. Seventy-five thousand dollars worth of the world's finest driving machinery, red as the blood that flows through my veins.

The owner of the company handed me the keys, I got in, and immediately drove to my parent's house in LA to show off. I asked my dad if he had any music for me to listen to, and he gave me a Dire Straits cassette. I drove back to Phoenix on I-10.

This is a true story. Looking back, what I find interesting is that I wasn't amazed that someone had given me the keys to a Porsche 930 to drive as my own. It didn't occur to me that I had manifested what I wanted through the use of visualization. All I did was ask and I got what I asked for. When I hung the picture of the Porsche on the wall, I wasn't feeling anxious, or wondering how I was going to get it, or worried that I wouldn't. I just hung it there, thinking that it was a cool thing to do, visualizing myself driving this car and having fun doing it.

There's more to the story.

The car was not given to me. The owner (a multi-millionaire) leased it and gave it to me to drive. It was my responsibility to come up with $1100 each month which included the insurance and the lease payment. That proved to be quite difficult for me.

Be Careful of What You Ask For

A few months later, in the parking lot of a pool hall where I was hanging out (a place few respectable Porsche owners would want to go), someone mangled the rear window wiper and kicked off the driver's motorized side view mirror. I didn't have the $350 deductible to replace them.

I was living in an apartment complex where I was parking a $75,000 car in the parking lot. One day someone smashed out the side window in a failed attempt to steal the car stereo. About a month later, I got a flat tire, but I couldn't afford to replace it so I drove around on the spare donut tire until I finally turned the car back in to the owner, a mere six months after I got it. The car was in sorry shape and I was glad to be done with it.

The Moral of the Story

What I should have asked for was an income that allowed me to own a Porsche. Instead, I asked to drive one down I-10 listening to a Dire Straits cassette, which I did. **I got what I asked for.**

Fast forward to this Monday, January 25th. I'm looking at my hypnotherapy appointments for the week and things are looking slow. I'm feeling just bit of anxiety, to be honest with you. I check my email and someone I haven't talked to in a long time sends me a link to a Tony Robbins* video. (Yes, I know I mention Robbins a lot, keep reading and you'll see why.) It's a really good video where Robbins talks about the use of "incantations", which are affirmations with lots of emotion. I wrote down verbatim one that he uses, and it goes like this: *"The abundance of God's wealth is circulating in my life. Its wealth flows to me in avalanches of abundance. All my needs and desires and goals are met instantaneously by Infinite Intelligence where I am one with God and God is everything. "*

After writing this down and tweaking it a bit to match my personal belief system, I proclaimed my version of this affirmation with all the passion and energy I could muster. I also added, *"My passion is helping people. People that I can help are calling me for hypnotherapy appointments."*

Within two hours two people called me to book appointments. A coincidence? Perhaps, but it didn't feel like it.

Why are we so afraid to ask for what we want and what we need?

As children we ask incessantly for what we want. Then we grow up, learn how we think the world really works, and stop asking because of disappointment, resignation, cynicism, fear of rejection and disappointment. Some of us are even taught, "If someone offers to give you something, you should politely decline."

What if everyone started asking, or even demanding, what they wanted, including: an end to poverty and war, quality schools, a working health care system, health, wealth, happiness, love?

Maybe it's all true: **Ask and you will receive.** *Knock and the door will be opened. Think and grow rich. What you focus on expands. When you visualize you materialize. The hows are the domain of the universe. Energy goes where attention flows. You become what you think about.*

I think I'm going back to being naive. I'm going to start to consider the following, not as truths, yet, but as possibilities:

- I can get what I want/need even though I might not deserve it.
- I can ask over and over again for what I want / need because I might just get it.
- I can get what I want/need even if I don't have the money for it.
- I might not have to work hard for what I want and need. Maybe I'll get it just because I asked nicely for it.
- I can take action to get what I want/need even if I don't do it perfect.
- The Universe, God, Infinite Intelligence, whatever you want to call it, wants to help me get what I want and need.
- Maybe, just maybe, I am the Creative Power in the flesh. Maybe I do have the power to manifest whatever I want quickly, possibly instantaneously and I just don't know it.
- Maybe I don't have to worry. Maybe I just need to ask and believe. Maybe worry and anxiety is the problem when I perceive that I'm not getting what I want.

It's not easy to train your mind to have faith in your ability to create what you want when it looks like it's not going to happen for you. But I'm in training. I'll let you know how it goes.

To learn more about Tony Robbins go to www.TonyRobbins.com

"Ask and you shall receive."

"Being comfortable speaking in front of a group is a skill you can learn."

Public Speaking: A Fear Worse Than Death?

In 1987 (the year of the Porsche) I was the general manager of an in-home sales company in Phoenix, Arizona. We would hire salespeople through what is known as "cattle calls": we'd run a newspaper ad to instruct everyone interested in the job to show up on Mondays at noon. My job was to stand up in front of these prospective salespeople and pitch them on how they could make a bunch of money selling our product in people's homes. Speaking in front of a group of people was not difficult for me. I was driving a nice car, making some money and feeling pretty good.

Well, as sometimes happens, **I fell into a slump** and my sales suddenly dropped off. It seemed like I couldn't sell a dollar for 50 cents. My boss was saying stuff like "I'd make more money by firing you". My confidence was at an all time low.

It was about then that we hired a kid named Jimmy. The first day out in the sales field, "Top Jimmy" sold three out of three appointments. He was confident and a smooth talker. Everyone loved Jimmy, while I was feeling like last year's model. To add insult to injury, within a few weeks he replaced me as general manager because of his stellar sales performance.

It was now his job to stand in front of a room filled with job hunters and give them the good news. He declined, and asked for a few more weeks to perfect his talk. I continued to do the "opportunity speech" for him, but I noticed that Jimmy was in no hurry to get up and do it.

One day when I was scheduled to do the speech, I came in to the office with a bad attitude because my sales were so dismal. The boss took a look at me and said "Moreno, there's no way you're going out in front of those people. Jimmy, get out there and do your stuff." From the look on Jimmy's face, I could see my suspicions were confirmed: **Top Jimmy was having some anxiety about speaking in public.**

Jimmy went out there in front of those 50 or so people and began the spiel. He started to stutter. He began to sweat profusely. His face was white. Then he just stopped, and I saw him go from being Top Jimmy to Top Ramen. He looked over to me desperately and said "Ted, why don't you take over..." He stepped down and I stepped up, both literally and figuratively. Jimmy never really recovered from the blow to his confidence. His sales fell and it wasn't long before he quit. My sales went back up and I regained my place as general manager.

It's been said that fear of public speaking is a fear worse than death for some people. Although I'm not sure how many people would rather take a bullet than be made to speak in public, it's a fact that many folks consider speaking in front of a group on par with a root canal on a list of their favorite activities. The sad part about Jimmy's plight was that even though I had no training as a coach or hypnotherapist at the time, had he asked, I probably could've helped him.

Nobody is born a good public speaker. As with all fears, anxiety about public speaking is learned, and what is learned can be unlearned. When someone says "I'm not a good speaker" all they are really saying is "I haven't developed the skills to be an effective speaker." Being comfortable speaking in front of a group is a skill you can learn.

Chances are that you'll be called upon to speak to a group at some point in your life. In today's business environment, you will almost certainly be required to give reports or presentations to colleagues or clients. If so, consider learning to speak in public as a necessary part of your personal and professional development.

If you are someone who gets the fight or flight response (sweaty palms, rapid heartbeat, shallow breathing, inability to think clearly) when asked to speak to a group, the good news is that you can learn to overcome the fear response and do a decent job. It doesn't have to be stressful. Many people who were once terrified to speak in public have gone on to become very good speakers. Here are some other things to remember:

You don't have to be a master orator in order to be effective. You just need to be yourself. Don't try to be or think of yourself as a "public speaker".

The audience is on your side, wanting you to succeed.

The chances of you loudly passing gas, fainting, throwing up, totally forgetting what you were going to say or the audience throwing stuff at you rarely happens and if it does, you can probably make a joke out of it.

You don't need to memorize a lot of information or even impart a lot of information. That's what notes and handouts are for.

It's ok to feel a little nervous, that's natural. You can learn to be ok with a little.

Of course, there are different levels of anxiety and fear when it comes to speaking to groups of people. On one end of the spectrum, you might be challenged by **social anxiety disorder** to the point where even talking to someone one on one is a problem. On the other end, you may feel fear or nervousness that makes the prospect of speaking just another stressful thing in your life. **Either way, if you need some help, give me a call.** Here are a few tips that you might find helpful the next time someone says "Get out there and do your stuff."

- **Practice but don't over-prepare**. Have an outline for what you are going to say. Put your notes on 3x5 index cards that are numbered in order. Practice saying the words out loud. Practice in front of someone you trust that can give you some feedback. Record yourself to see what vocal tics you might want to work with. Practice in front of a mirror.
- **Don't be boring**. The worst sin you can commit as a speaker is making people wish they were somewhere else. Although there are many situations where one may need to speak, try to craft your message to your audience so that what you tell them has some impact on them.
- **Humor is good.** People want to laugh, and when they do, you'll feel a lot more comfortable. Just use common sense to avoid offending your audience.
- **Humility is good.** Don't try to come across as an expert if you aren't. Even if you are, remember, people don't care how much you know unless they know how much you care. (I love that one.)

- **Make sure you eat something**. Diet and your level of anxiety are intimately related. Don't go in front of a group on an empty stomach or over-caffeinated.
- **Monitor the conversation in your head** so that it supports you. It doesn't help to say things like "I just know I'm going to screw this up." or "I hate this". Be realistic in your expectations and show this in your language to yourself. "I can do this, it's only ten minutes" or "This is a great opportunity to show my stuff."

My job is not to teach you how to become an effective speaker, but to help you manage or let go of the fear and anxiety that you might have. There's a lot of material out there that can teach you to be a good public speaker including books, DVDs and audio programs. Toastmasters is the most well known and respected venue for people to hone their skills, and I highly recommend that you check out your local chapter.

If public speaking is scary to you, come to believe that rather than die, you can learn to be comfortable whenever you're called upon to "show your stuff."

"The audience is on your side, wanting you to succeed."

"The only time you are actually growing is when you are uncomfortable."

How Uncomfortable Can You Get?

At the bottom of the Grand Canyon I was camping out with about 30 other people on a river rafting trip with Arizona River Runners.* My best buddy Brian is the senior boatman for ARR, and I was working the trip as a swamper, which is basically an unpaid helper to Brian and the other river guides on the 2 boats of our 9 day trip.

On one evening of the trip, Brian and I were cleaning up after dinner while the passengers were pitching their tents. Suddenly, one of the passengers came running up to tell us that someone had spotted a rattlesnake close to the passengers' tents. Brian grabbed his "snake tool" and we headed off to capture the snake to relocate him to another part of the beach for no other reason than to calm down some very frightened passengers who had never seen a rattlesnake, much less had to share a beach with one.

The snake decided that the best place to be was hidden deep in the brush and try as we might, we couldn't get close enough to snag it, not that we really wanted to. We assured the very concerned passengers that snakes would rather avoid people and that this snake was surely going to get as far away from this mass of humanity as possible.

After the trip ended, one woman confided to us that she got so freaked out about the snake that she had decided to stop drinking water so that she would become dehydrated and have to get helicoptered out of the canyon. Temperatures at the bottom of the canyon can get as high as 120 degrees in the summer, so if you don't drink water, you can bet that you will get dehydrated and incur the $1500 cost of being flown out to the nearest hospital on the rim.

She had a choice: **possibly risk her life by allowing dehydration and pay for evacuation from a trip for which she had already spent a good chunk of money, or face her discomfort to experience a once in a lifetime adventure**.

She chose to stick it out. She came to realize that *to experience the beauty and majesty of the Grand Canyon from a boat on the river, she would have to endure some discomfort.*

Like any wilderness expedition, a river trip down the Canyon involves blazing heat, sleeping on the ground, no shower or public facilities, and an array of wildlife including poisonous snakes. Still, she said that it was one of the most incredible experiences of her life and that she wanted to do it again. **She decided that she could be comfortable with being uncomfortable.**

How many opportunities for growth have you passed up because there was going to be some discomfort involved? How many exciting adventures have you missed out on? How much of the really good stuff of life have you left behind because you didn't want to experience some discomfort?

Consider that the only time you are actually growing is when you are uncomfortable. Where you are now in your life, financially, physically, mentally, spiritually and emotionally, is within your comfort zone. **To grow, to learn and to change, you need to step out of that comfort zone and get uncomfortable.**

It's not easy to do or try something you've never done before, like camping or learning a new language. It won't feel right, you won't be doing it perfect, you will feel out of place, and it might not be what you thought. However, with a little consistency and by doing it regularly, something interesting happens: It starts to get easier. If you persist, something amazing happens. It becomes very comfortable to do and possibly uncomfortable not to.

This is how habits are formed, by allowing your (subconscious) mind to get comfortable with something new by walking through the initial discomfort. Think about the things you want to do or try but haven't, like starting an exercise program, taking a class, going on a trip, introducing yourself to someone or joining a club or organization. *Is it the discomfort of the unknown that's stopping you?* If so, here are some things to think about to move you in the direction of embracing discomfort for progress, change, growth or learning.

Life is not always comfortable. Duh! Even if you try to make it so, discomfort will come along for no other reason than you are alive. Even if you could stay in your jammies in bed watching TV all day, you'd still get hungry, bored, etc. What kind of life is that anyway?

There are presently areas of your life where you already accept discomfort because there is a great payoff in doing so. Example: getting up to go to work, going to the dentist.

Discomfort by itself won't kill you. It might make you grumpy, angry, scared, or nervous, but rarely does anyone die from discomfort.

You need discomfort. That's how life gets your attention. It makes you take action even if you don't want to. e.g." I don't have time to eat but I'm so hungry I can't think straight."

Discomfort makes like worth living. Uncertainty is uncomfortable. But if all you ever had was certainty in your life, you might do something to screw it up and create uncertainty to make life interesting. (People do it all the time, e.g. creating drama.)

You can feel uncomfortable and not let it stop you. When you are uncomfortable in a new situation, simply acknowledge that to yourself. "I'm uncomfortable but I don't need to let it stop me."

The reason hypnotherapy is effective in creating change is that it help your mind become comfortable with the new and unfamiliar. But you can do it on your own as well. Just see every time you feel uncomfortable as an opportunity for learning. Love discomfort! Embrace it! Welcome it! If you are uncomfortable, it simply means you are alive and growing.

For more information about the Grand Canyon trips that Arizona River Runners offers, go to www.raftarizona.com.

"We play scary movies in our head over and over."

Would You Get an Oscar for Your Mind Movies?

The Academy Awards* is coming to TV screens all over America this month. Here in the Los Angeles area where I live, it's a really big deal.

If you look back at the **winners of the Oscar over the past 20 years** you'll see that more than half of the winners for Best Motion Picture are about the incredible ability of the human spirit to triumph over adversity and our own human weaknesses. We like going to the movies but we love to be moved and inspired by them. Movies like *Slumdog Millionaire, Crash, Million Dollar Baby, Lord of the Rings, Gladiator, Titanic, Braveheart, Forrest Gump, and Schindler's List* move us with themes of redemption, heroism, hope, and triumph.

On the other hand, have you ever walked out of a movie feeling like you got **ripped off?** Like you were expecting something interesting or great to happen and **nothing happened?** Or you walked out of a film feeling like you really didn't need to see what they showed you? What about a movie that leaves you **worried or anxious?** Would you go see that film again and again and again?

Yet, in a way, that's what many of us have a tendency to do. We play scary movies in our head over and over. Angst- filled mind movies with themes such as loss, hurt, pain, failure, futility, desperation and hopelessness.

So what about the movies in your head? Are you currently running an inspiring tale of adventure and victory like *Lawrence of Arabia* or is it a big budget disaster film like *Towering Inferno*? Would you get an Academy Award for the stories you consistently tell yourself or would you get a big fat Razzie, the award given to the cheesiest movies of the year? I call these stories in our heads **Mind Movies.**

Like a film in a cinema, these pictures in your mind will affect you, either positive or negative. The only difference is that you usually don't go to see the same film in a theatre every day. But your mind movies are always with you. And in a large part they can determine your level of happiness and success in life. If you run scary and frightening scenarios in your mind then that's how you're going to feel. On the other hand, if you can create pictures in your head of you overcoming challenges and steadfastly moving forward in the direction of your heart's desire then you will feel hopeful and energized.

You are not only the theatre owner, determining what films will be shown in your mind's theater, but you are also the director and editor of your mind movies. Ask yourself, what are the scenes in my head doing for me and my life? Are they serving me? Or are they keeping me in a constant negative state by scaring the spit out of me? (Ever been so scared your mouth went dry? That's what I'm talking about.)

If what you see in your head is not keeping you inspired and hopeful, then pull that reel off quick and put something else on that big screen! Here are some tips to get you started.

- **Practice visualizing what you want**. First thing in the morning and last thing at night, imagine yourself accomplishing your goal. Put a grand and moving soundtrack to it. This is the actual process of making your own Mind Movies that move you in direction you want to go. It doesn't take very long, but it's powerful. *It's a form of self-hypnosis.*
- **Get out a pen and paper and write the screenplay for your compelling mind movie.** What is the story that you most want told about you and your life? Make it exciting and inspiring.
- **Go out and rent movies that make you feel good**. There are so many films out there that tell amazing stories of people overcoming the most incredible challenges. Have you even noticed that after you watch a really impactful movie it stays in your head for a while? That can be a really good thing.
- **Watch stuff that makes you laugh.** Laughter is good medicine for what ails you.
- **Create a vision board.** Cut out pictures from magazines and catalogs of what you want and what you want to do. Make a collage on a bulletin board or firm poster board. Put a cut out photo of your head on the bodies of people doing fabulous things.
- **Avoid watching stuff that brings you down!** How many times do you have to be reminded? How much news do you really need?

Remember, images are the language of the subconscious mind, the seat of your deepest habits and though patterns. Whatever images you hold consistently in your mind have a tendency to show up in your life. If the Mind Movies you are watching in your head are the type that go straight to video and then end up on the supermarket rack, then give me a call and I'll give you a ticket to a better film using the magic of hypnotherapy.

When you imagine yourself on that stage receiving the Oscar for your amazing story of how you emerged victorious in the face of overwhelming odds, I hope that I'm on your thank you list.

ACADEMY AWARD(S) ®, OSCAR(S) ®, OSCAR NIGHT® and OSCAR® statuette design mark are the registered trademarks and service marks, and the OSCAR® statuette the copyrighted property, of the Academy of Motion Picture Arts and Sciences.

Slumdog Millionaire (2008) Distributor: Fox Searchlight Pictures

Crash (2004) Distributor: Lions Gate Films

Million Dollar Baby (2004) Distributor: Warner Bros.

The Lord of the Rings: The Fellowship of the Ring (2001) Distributor: New Line Cinema

Gladiator (2000) Distributor: DreamWorks

Titanic (1997) Distributor: Paramount Pictures

Braveheart (1995) Distributor: Paramount Pictures

Forrest Gump (1994) Distributor: Paramount Pictures

Schindler's List (1993) Distributor: Universal Pictures

Lawrence of Arabia (1962) Distributor: Columbia Pictures

Towering Inferno (1974) Distributor: 20th Century Fox

"The greatest skill you will ever learn is how to control your thinking."

Who Has Control of Your Mind?

It's still surprising to me how many people out there are afraid of hypnosis and hypnotherapy. It happens all the time: when I tell someone I'm a hypnotherapist, they put their hand in front of their face and exclaim *"Don't look at me!"* Believe it or not, I've actually had people ask me *"Are you hypnotizing me now?"* Other times, people say *"I would never allow someone to control my mind."* I have to chuckle inside. What they are telling me is that they would be an excellent hypnosis subject because they believe I can control their mind. Of course, that is simply not true.

My job is not to control your mind but to help *you* get control of your own mind. I have to remind myself occasionally that there is still a lot of fear and misinformation out there about what hypnosis is and isn't. As a hypnotherapist, it's easy to assume that everyone is aware of the value of hypnotherapy. In fact, most people are not.

When I say controlling your mind I mean controlling your thoughts. That's why people come to me: they are having trouble controlling their thoughts. Thoughts lead to behavior. Their thoughts and behaviors are not getting them what they want. Make sense? *I help people to have control over their minds so that they are thinking the thoughts and doing the things that help them get what they want and feel the way they want to feel.*

Do you use a washboard to wash your clothes? You might not even know what a washboard is. Yet there was a time when most folks used a washboard to wash their clothes. Hardly anybody uses a washboard anymore because we now have a better tool: a washing machine.

Hypnosis is simply a tool, but a very effective and powerful tool. In my opinion, it's the tool of the future when it comes to tapping your potential. It may be called auto-suggestion, reprogramming, or guided visualization, but the goal is the same: to de-hypnotize yourself from the control of limiting beliefs and bad habits that keep you from moving forward in your life.

If you are a long time reader of my blog, you may have heard this before. But it bears repeating that **all hypnosis is self-hypnosis.** Here are some other points to remember if **you are thinking about using hypnotherapy to help you achieve your goals.**

Hypnosis is based on <u>science.</u>

Hypnosis is a natural state we all go into, pretty much on a daily basis. If you've ever missed your off ramp because you were "spacing out" then you know what it feels like to be in trance state.

It's all about the power of suggestion. I simply guide you into a state you've been in many times before, this time under controlled conditions where I give you suggestions based on what you've told me you want to change or achieve. You are very open to suggestions (suggestible) when you are in hypnosis.

Since it's a natural state, everyone can be hypnotized. The fact is, there are a lot of people out there already walking around in a trance.

Ever seen a stage hypnosis show? People ask me all the time if it's real. It is real and yes, those people are really under hypnosis. How does the hypnotist get them to do wacky things? Well for starters, they volunteer! They know what to expect. The fact that they raise their hands to volunteer means they expect to get hypnotized. Still, some don't really allow it to happen and they get sent back to their seats.

Here is something to ponder: you are already hypnotized to act and behave in certain ways, even if you don't want to. It's called social conditioning, or the hypnosis of the culture.

I've heard it said and I agree that the greatest skill you will ever learn is how to control your thinking. Hypnotherapy is an excellent tool for doing that. If you know someone who has tried over and over to change something in their life but have not succeeded, it might be time for them to get a better tool. Have them give me a call!

"Hypnosis is simply a very effective and powerful tool."

"A daily practice of meditation can be profound and life changing."

A Technique for Stress Relief That is Thousands of Years Old

I believe that the most powerful force on the planet is the human mind. However, instead of using our minds to create our lives, many of us are controlled by our own minds. The most obvious result of being controlled by your mind is stress. I'd like to suggest one technique to help you get control over your mind and that is meditation or awareness practice.

I won't bore you with statistics regarding how stress can kill you or how stress related diseases are the number one killer of Americans. And you know that we cannot avoid stress. A certain amount of stress is good and needed to keep us alive.

In our modern culture, though, the amount of stress we experience can be crushing. Much of our stress comes from thoughts of fear and worry:

- How am I ever going to...
- I have to....
- I really need to...
- This sucks...
- I can't believe this is happening...
- I hate this...I can't stand this...I'm sick of this...
- Why does this always happen...
- I can't deal with this...
- What if (this bad thing happens)

Meditation is a powerful way to deal with stress. When you read the word meditation, you might think of someone sitting in the lotus position chanting "Om". You might think meditation refers to a particular religious belief system. It is much more than that. I have sat in Zen meditation alongside Catholic nuns and priests.

Meditation means awareness. Awareness of what your mind is doing. You are present to what is going on now.

When we become aware of what our mind is thinking, then we can have detachment. Detachment allows us to see our stressful thoughts for what they really are: stressful thoughts making us stressed. This gives us the opportunity to choose what we think. This is the beginning of true freedom. We can learn to stop worrying ourselves or scaring ourselves to death, or at least, ill-health.

A daily practice of meditation can be profound and life changing. You may not have time or the desire to develop a daily practice. That's fine. What I'd like to do is give you a few simple things to do that can be very helpful when you are feeling stressed out.

Basic technique: close your eyes and take some deep breaths while focusing on your breathing. Breathe deeply into your abdomen. This can be done just about anywhere, anytime. Try it right now. You'll notice a change right away. You can say something to yourself, such as "I'm ok" or "calm" or "relax". What you are doing is taking your mind off of what is causing you stress and focusing on NOW. Just for a few minutes, let go of the outside world.

While driving: ... please don't close your eyes! See if you can let go of wanting your traffic situation to be different. Be present to what is. Most people drive unconsciously, their minds a million miles away. Try driving consciously. If you are stressed, turn off the radio or music. Notice the color of the car in front of you. Notice your surroundings, where are you? Notice the sky, the trees, the landscape.

A more formal way to meditate: before bed or right after waking up, sit in a chair. Try to keep you back straight. Breathe deeply and count your breaths, starting with each inhale. Count to 10, then start over. Do it for 5 minutes. If you can't do it for 5 minutes, do it for 3 minutes, or 1 minute.

Focus on an object. It might be the flame of a candle, or a flower in a vase. Sitting on a bench in a park, it might be a tree. Breathe and simply focus on an object without trying to describe it, categorize it or have an opinion about it.

Devotional meditation. It's said that when you pray you talk to Spirit and when you meditate you listen. You can focus on Divine Love, simply allowing yourself to feel it. Or you might focus on a religious icon or a picture of a divine being.

Don't worry about doing it right. The point is to get in the habit of letting go of the stressful thoughts, going inside and getting centered and grounded.

If you are interested in creating a regular mediation practice, I encourage and support you. Hypnotherapy can be helpful in developing the determination and motivation to practice. If you have questions or would like some coaching regarding meditation, feel free to call me for a free half hour consultation.

"Things do not always go according to plan."

Life is Hard But That Doesn't Mean That You Suck

One day many years ago, I was packing up my clothes to move out of a house that I had been renting with a girlfriend. We were breaking up and I was deeply depressed. This scenario had happened all too often in my life, another failed relationship. The effort it took to pack up my stuff felt crushing and immense. At one point I sat on my bed, despondent and unable to continue.

Just at that moment the phone rang. It was a healer, an older woman who I had been seeing for some physical problems. Hearing the anguish in my voice, she asked me what was wrong. I told her and finished with a pleading and desperate question: **"This is not the first time this has happened, what is wrong with me?"**

She said, **"There is nothing wrong with you, dear. We all have certain challenges that we must deal with. Life is hard sometimes, but you'll get through this."** I did get through it, and I moved into a happier and more peaceful place, both literally and emotionally.

Life is hard sometimes. But here's the important thing to remember: Just because life is hard doesn't mean that there is something wrong with you.

There is a book by David Richo called *The Five Things We Cannot Change (and the Happiness We Find by Embracing Them.)* The five things are:

- Everything changes and ends.
- Things do not always go according to plan.
- Life is not always fair.
- Pain is a part of life.
- People are not loving and loyal all the time.

So much insanity and deep unhappiness comes from believing that life should be different from what it is. And when it doesn't turn out the way we think it should, it's easy to feel that we are completely to blame. We can be so invested in "doing it right" and "looking good" that when we fall short of our own or other's expectations we make it mean that there is something wrong with us, that we are no good, or that we are in need of fixing.

What does it mean when life is painful, when the plan falls apart, when people betray you? Well, first and foremost, it means you're alive and probably human. It might also mean that there are things you need to learn. How to make better choices, perhaps. More careful planning. Greater consideration about who you decide to associate with. How do you learn this stuff? Well, mainly by screwing up. Life's a joker, ain't she?

I don't feel *too* bad when my car breaks down and I'm unable to fix it on my own. It's not a skill I've acquired and I'm not really interested in learning. But when the money is not coming in as fast as I want or need, the *"I suck"* conversation comes up pretty quick! But it doesn't mean that I suck, it just means I need to learn more about creating wealth. I can be OK with that, and then make the choice to learn. But it's hard to be OK *with "I'm not earning what I think I should earn, so there must be something wrong with me"*.

Once we accept that life is hard, once we accept and embrace the five things we cannot change, then the only question is "What am I going to do about it?" It's a much better question than "What is wrong with me?" or "Why is this happening to me?"

Of course, you can always answer the question "What am I going to do about it?' with "Nothing! That's why I suck!" or I don't know how.., I can't.., I'm afraid..,It's too hard... But these responses are not very empowering.

Let me suggest some powerful responses to the question "What am I going to do about it?" when life gets hard.

- I'll do what I can do.
- I can't do anything, so I'll accept that this is going to be tough and I'll just get tougher.

- I can't do anything, so I'll just have myself a good cry and carry on.
- Nothing. I choose powerfully to do nothing until I choose to do something. I'm willing to accept the consequences of doing nothing.
- Who can I ask for help?
- How can I learn to deal with this effectively?
- A challenge! Cool. I love challenges.
- What doesn't kill me makes me stronger.
- Life is getting hard. Interesting. I'll use this experience to: write my blog/song/book/paint my masterpiece/help other people going through what I'm going through.
- Are you kidding? I'm a friggin' Master of the Universe! These puny challenges are nothing compared to the stuff that's going to come up when I'm playing really big!

Life will be hard sometimes regardless of what you believe about yourself. However, if deep down inside you carry the belief that you are up to dealing with life when it gets hard, then you can turn "Life is hard" into "That's life".

* Richo, David *The Five Things We Cannot Change (and the Happiness We Find by Embracing Them.)* 2006 Shambhala

"Love yourself."

Might Be the Hardest Thing You'll Ever Learn

Chris Whitley, one of my favorite musical artists, does a cover of an old standard that I really like. The name of the song is "Nature Boy."* The last line of the song goes like this:

"The greatest thing
You'll ever learn
Is just to love
And be loved
In return"

Loving, being loving, is not easy, and that's an understatement. Being loved in return, being able to accept love, might be just as difficult for some. But to be able to fully love and be loved in return, you must learn what might be the most difficult thing you'll ever learn, and that is to **love yourself.**

Mention "loving yourself" in social conversation and you'll either get snickers or an uncomfortable silence, depending on the company you keep. The importance of self-love is like an iceberg, immense, yet so hidden. To ask the question *"Do I love myself?"* cuts deep down to our very perception of whom and what we are. If we even get an inkling about the extent of our own self acceptance and self-love, it's usually due to the lack of it.

It's no wonder. Self loathing is such an epidemic in our modern culture, it's almost fashionable. The Flawed Hero or Anti-Hero is our current popular icon. Dr. House, Jason Bourne, Dexter, Jack Bauer. Even Spiderman's a nerd.

Yet, the fact remains, and it's indisputable. **You can only love another and accept love to the extent that you love and accept yourself.**

What keeps us from loving and accepting ourselves? Many things. Negative conditioning from the past, resentments against ourselves for past failures, negative conditioning from the culture at large. Watch the news.

Violence, war, death, murder, betrayal, dishonesty, cheating, lying, greed. It's hard not to come away with the belief that people are terrible, and since I am people, I must be terrible. **Do you see the subliminal programming taking place here?**

So what do we do? How do we overcome any dislike, judgment or even loathing for ourselves? How do we learn to love and accept ourselves for who we are as well as who we are not?

Start by separating who you are from what you do. Here's the thing that makes it so very difficult. You cannot base your love and acceptance of yourself on what you do. In other words, you can't say *"I love myself only when I do good things."* That's called conditional love. It implies that if I do a bad thing, it all goes out the window. Other examples:

- I'll love and accept myself as long as I'm winning.
- I'll love and accept myself as long as I'm kind and generous.
- I'll love and accept myself when I feel good about myself.
- I'll love and accept myself when there is someone around to tell me they love me.
- I'll love and accept myself when I 'm doing it right, living up to my expectations, etc.

See the problem with these? Love and acceptance for yourself is not created in the conversation "I love and accept myself because of these reasons..." It comes out of the following conversation:

"I love and accept myself for who I am: a being whose nature is to love, who is capable of love. I don't need a reason to love and accept myself. I love myself because I choose to. Period." Like I said, this may be the hardest thing you will ever learn. Sadly, many people never learn.

If I stand in the place of "I love and accept myself unconditionally" then I have love to give and I am more aware of when I am not loving to others. I accept my humanity and the fact that I will screw up, make mistakes, hurt people. I can forgive myself, and thus, have a greater capacity to forgive others. I see that when others are hurtful, petty and mean that they are being challenged by their own self dislike, and then I can have compassion, because I have been there.

You might ask, "Should I love and accept myself if I am doing terrible things?" I would suggest that if someone is doing terrible things they are doing it out of their own self loathing. If I have truly learned to love myself, then I honor myself. To cheat you, to betray you, to inflict violence upon you, dishonors me, dishonors the highest ideal I hold for myself. That ideal is to be loving to all, starting with myself.

We will fall short of our ideal as humans do. Yet in my experience, it's the inability to accept that we will fall short, and the judgment that results, that begins to blind us to the inner light of our own magnificence.

Keep your flame alive. Refuse to tear yourself down or beat yourself up. Forgive yourself or ask for forgiveness. Tell yourself daily "I'm ok and doing the best I can." Strive as much as possible to be honest with yourself. Learn to love yourself and accept yourself while knowing that there is always room for improvement. The greatest things to learn are often the hardest.

* "Nature Boy" (written by Eden Ahbez, 1947) Recorded by Chris Whitley and released on the album *War Crime Blues* (2004), Messenger Records

"It takes courage to look in someone's eyes because to do that you must reveal yourself."

Please Look In To My Eyes

A number of years ago I did a self-development seminar called the Landmark Forum.* It was a life changing experience for me, and even though it's not for everyone, I highly recommend that you check it out.

One of the exercises we did during the seminar was to stand across from another person and look into their eyes for five minutes without saying anything. When the exercise was announced, I heard someone sitting behind me say "What a stupid exercise. I look into people's eyes all day long; I don't need to pay to do it in a seminar."

I'd never done this sort of exercise but I thought it might be interesting. Well, it was a lot more interesting than I thought.

I stood across from my partner in the exercise and looked into their eyes. Immediately, a conversation started in my head, and it went something like this:

"God, this is weird, I don't even know this person and now I'm staring into their eyes. This is a little embarrassing. I wonder what they think about me. Geez, I hope I don't have any eye boogers. Should I smile? If I start to smile, I might start laughing. That wouldn't be cool because they might think I was laughing at them. Now they're smiling at me. What does that mean? How much time has passed? When do we break for lunch?"

Some people did start laughing, little nervous laughs. Then some people started crying, one of whom was the woman who thought the exercise was stupid.

The conversation in my head started to quiet down. I stopped thinking about me and started to think about them. What were they like? What did they do? I thought I saw some sadness in their eyes. What had happened to them?

Then something very interesting happened. The conversation in my head stopped and I found myself with another human being. Not doing, not talking, just being with them. Without knowing any of the details of their life, I realized that I knew everything about them that I needed to know. I felt connected with them, and it felt comfortable, and, well, good. It was an incredibly powerful experience.

When the exercise was over, the woman who complained shared her experience with the group. She said *"I wept because I realized I never look into anybody's eyes. Even when I'm in front of someone, I'm never really with them."*

I've had the opportunity to do this exercise in workshops more than once and each time I'm blown away by the experience.

It makes me aware that many of us, me included, have the tendency to go through the day in a way that is closed off and sealed tight. Eyes averted, face stiff and hard. "Let's get this over with asap" we say with our body language. Sometimes at networking events, when I shake someone's hand they're not even looking at me.

We come into contact every day with so many people but often it's no more personal or meaningful than getting a soda out of a vending machine. Sometimes I'm aware of talking with my children without even looking at them and the talking is automatic. "Yes, oh, that's nice, yeah, uh huh, ok..."

It takes courage to look in someone's eyes because to do that you must reveal yourself. You let the other person in a little. You let them "see" you. This is can be threatening for some people.

But **when I remember to look into the eyes of another, then every contact is an opportunity for connection with another.** You might think this would get exhausting, but the amazing thing is that it gives me energy, a feeling of lightness. I acknowledge them, and they, me.

When I stop what I'm doing and look into the eyes of my children, I become present to their innocence, their beauty and their incredible aliveness. And I get some of that for myself.

We're all trying to feel better and be happier. We're all trying to feel less isolated in the solitary but cramped spaces of our minds.

Try this just for today: look into the eyes of each person you come into contact with. See what comes up. Discomfort? Self consciousness? Maybe you're already good at connecting with people in this manner. If so, then notice how many people have trouble meeting your gaze.

If we could learn to look into each other's eyes with respect, acceptance and compassion, then we just might see the soul behind those windows. Then perhaps we would see each other for who we really are: vast, infinite, limitless and magnificent.

For more information about Landmark Education, go to www.landmarkeducation.com

"Stop Complaining."

Don't Let Them In! Five Steps for Keeping the Mental Mischief Makers Away

I hate to admit this to you, but when I was younger and much more foolish, I used to open my door to some pretty unsavory characters.

They weren't even very likable, I just got comfortable having them around. They were familiar and I knew what to expect from them. I didn't realize until much later how much hanging around with them was holding me back from what I knew I could be.

One day, there was a knock on the door while I was reading a book by the first self-development author I ever read, Dr. Wayne Dyer. I opened the door to find **Cynicism**, someone I knew very well, standing there. I was dismayed to see that he had brought **Negativity** with him, who I really despised, especially since he was always wearing that dumb "I'm With Stupid" T-shirt.

"Hey dude. It's another crappy day. Perfect day for getting messed up", Cynicism said. I noticed he had brought along a six pack of his favorite beverage, Notwieser Light.

I don't know why, maybe it was the Dyer book, but I said "Sorry guys, not today".

Negativity stepped forward and whined "Don't be like that, homey! Let's throw back a few and complain about the system!"

I hate being called homey. "No", I said. "You guys get outta here. Now. I'm busy."

They shuffled off, Cynicism grumbling "Thinks he's too good now..."

I sat back down and felt weird. This was uncomfortable for me. I've always been a "nice" guy. I pretty much let in whoever wanted to come in and let them stay as long as they wanted.

Right then, there was another knock at the door. I got up, irritated. I threw open the door expecting Negativity and Cynicism but instead, **Possibility** was standing there. I'd seen him a couple of times, but didn't really know him too well. "Hey", he said."I thought I would drop by since I was in the neighborhood. Mind if I come in?"

"Sure", I replied. "But tell me, what kept you from coming by before?"

"I've tried" he said. "But I make it a point not to hang out with those other two clowns who just left."

Cynicism and Negativity still come by and knock, but most of the time I just don't open the door and pretty soon they go away. The odd times that I do let them in because I'm too tired to say "Get lost"; I make sure they don't stay very long. I haven't seen **Resignation** and **Despair** in a while. I gave **Fear** my key one time but I'm in the process of changing the locks. More and more, I find myself entertaining Possibility, who is always welcome, along with **Hope, Belief,** and **Courage.** Needless to say, life is much better.

Here are five simple steps to keep those Mental Mischief Makers (MMMs) from messing with your mind.

Stop Complaining. The MMMs are attracted to complaining like ants to sugar. They seem to have some special radar to help them find complainers. First they'll allow you to feel justified, and then they'll move in and take over the place.

Plant gratitude outside your front door. You know how some animals will not come into your garden if you have the right herbs planted to keep them from eating your veggies? Gratitude is repellent to Negativity and in large enough amounts does a great job of keeping the other jokers away too.

Take regular Inspiration Vacations. Read, hear, and see things that inspire you. There's no way that you will even hear those troublemakers knock if you're involved in something that lifts you up and inspires you. Keep your mind in that place where your highest ideals reside.

Use Incantations. This is the magic that really acts like a spell to keep Negativity, Resignation, Fear, Cynicism, Doubt, and Despair away. Incantations are what you say to yourself to create what you want. Examples: I can do this, I have what it takes, I am up to this challenge, I am attracting money now, creativity flows through me. To make them really powerful, write them down and put them near a candle and light it. Seriously, I'm not kidding. Say these things a hundred times a day. **Really.**

Always be up to something. If you are up to stuff, making stuff happen, dreaming, hoping, planning, taking action, then you will be too busy for these those pesky MMMs when they come to visit. You'll see them for what they are: a distraction and a diversion from making your unique contribution to life.

*"Nothing is ever always
in balance."*

Your Life in Balance? Forget About It

A few weeks back I was hanging out with my two daughters, The Chick and Rock. It was a beautiful day in the San Gabriel valley, and on such days I like to take them to the park. That day, however, there were a lot of things on my to-do list.

My plan was to fix them lunch and plant them in front of the TV so I could get some work done. But the lovely day called to me, so we went outside and had a picnic in the backyard. They loved it. So did I, even if I didn't accomplish everything on my list. Those girls are always on my list.

Over the years, I've tried to divide my life into priorities and give equal attention to them all: my health, my work, my relationships, my spirituality, my social life and my alone time.

I've never been able to do it. There is always one area that needs more attention than another, and when that gets handled, then another area needs attention. If business is booming, then I haven't been taking my daily walk. If I'm feeling serene and peaceful because I'm taking alone time, then I probably haven't been spending enough time with my family.

Eventually, I realized that nothing is ever always in balance. It's a pendulum; it seems, swinging from one extreme to the other. And that's ok, because that's how life is: in balance for a minute, then out.

It's either moving toward summer or winter; when is it balanced? Only twice a year, on the summer and winter solstices. It's either day or night; when is it balanced? For a short time, twice a day, at dawn and dusk.

And why would you want to be balanced? If there is balance then there is no motion, no growth, and no progress. Balance is stasis, nothing is happening.

Life is a see-saw. One day you're up, the next, you're down.

Right now I'm in Apple Valley visiting my brother-in-law. There's a ton of stuff I need to do, including write this. If it was up to me, I'd be working all the time, but as a married guy, it's not totally up to me is it? So we're taking a weekend vacation. Keeps the wife happy, gives the kids a break from the routine, and gives me a chance to record some tunes in my brother-in-law's recording studio. So the pendulum swings to the other side, but I can be cool with that.

If you are one of those with lots of leisure time to devote to every part of your life, then lucky you! I remember those days. But if you're like me, trying to balance a career and a family with staying healthy and having some time for reflection, creativity and spirituality, then maybe balance isn't the answer.

Maybe the answer is to strive for being well-rounded and having a level of satisfaction that you can live with and be happy with in any particular area. Some areas are going to be more important or impactful than others. Those deserve more time and energy.

Here are some ideas that might be helpful:

Most of us have numerous roles, interests, and responsibilities which fit into distinct areas of life. Decide what these areas of importance are for you. These would be areas you feel you need to put time and energy into to have a successful and well-rounded life. An example would be the "Wheel of Life" consisting of Financial and Career, Family and Home, Spiritual and Ethical, Social and Cultural, Physical and Health, and Mental and Educational.

Rate these areas according to your current level of satisfaction and achievement in each. You might use a scale of 1-100 or 1-10.

What does this tell you? If you have always considered your health to be important but you rate it on the low side, then perhaps at this time health needs more of your attention then you are giving it. Maybe your financial house is well in order, you've got some cash in the bank and your score is high in this area. Consider that perhaps it's time to put some attention into another area that has a low score.

Create some goals based on those areas of importance that have lower levels of satisfaction and achievement. For example, if you feel that being a lifetime learner is important to you, and you have rated your Mental/Educational area on the low side, then you might think about taking class, reading a book, or taking an online course.

Revisit your areas of importance in six months. Has anything changed? Should you continue your present course of focus or is there another area that has become more important or meaningful to you in light of recent events in the past six months? Revisit twice a year.

For your car to get you where you want it to go, you need four good tires, good brakes, gas in your tank and a regular schedule of maintenance. You can ignore any of these for a while, but ignore any one of them for too long and you might soon be in trouble. Instead of striving for balance, just make sure you know what part of your life needs attention and you'll avoid being stranded by the side of the road.

"When two countries are ready to go to war, a group of moms from each country should meet in a neutral country to hash it out over coffee or tea."

New Rules I Think Should Be Implemented in Honor of Mothers

Today, Mother's Day, we celebrate the most important job in the world: Motherhood. So in honor of Mothers Day, I have some very radical suggestions that I think should be implemented immediately for the good of people kind as well as for the good of the planet. You may say I'm crazy, and it may be true, but I'll bet both of our moms back me on this one.

First, it should be required that all presidents, prime ministers and dictators of all countries be a mother. The second in command can be a dude, but the first in command should be a mom. They get a lot of stuff done in little time, and they're good at juggling numerous duties. They're also good at breaking up fights, which is really important these days. They should be allowed the liberal use of "time outs" for any rascally politicians caught acting out. They should be required to cook a home cooked meal for their staff once a month, with the staff washing the dishes. They also should be required to take a short vacation every month.

A law should be passed that half of all politicians in the US Senate and House be woman, preferably mothers. This would immediately raise the standards of behavior in these bodies. I went to an all- boy's high school, and believe me, it was a zoo. Without girls to act cool for, pretty much anything goes.

When two countries are ready to go to war, a group of moms from each country should meet in a neutral country to hash it out over coffee or tea. If they succeed in avoiding war, they get a weekend spa treatment.

There should be a governing Earth Mother Committee. This would be a group of older mothers who would be responsible for the care of the planet, including its animals. Anybody caught spilling oil, polluting, decimating animal populations or in any way messing up the global house would be spanked with a wooden spoon on international television.

Every city over 50,000 in population should have a "Mom of the Month". She should get preferred parking wherever she goes and get her picture in the newspaper. Oh, and a weekend spa treatment.

Psychotherapists should license a new type of therapist in addition to Marriage and Family Therapist (MFT) and Licensed Clinical Social Worker. (LCSW). This new type of therapist would be called a Maternal Orientation Modality Specialist (MOMS). You would go to this type of therapist to get a good talking-to or to get read the riot act. You could also go to get a big hug if you needed one.

Last but not least,and this is a big one, God shall be referred to from now on as Her. She would be known as the Heavenly Mother. I think we can agree that God can be anything She wants to be: woman, man, mother or father, so why not let the Mother thing run for a while? Seems only fair.

This post is in honor of my Grandmother who passed away recently, and in honor of all mothers who have left us.

~Happy Mother's Day to those we are lucky to still have with us.

"This chapter is in honor of my Grandmother who passed away recently, and in honor of all mothers who have left us."

"Many people are looking for someone to teach and guide them."

Things I Learned From My Dad

My dad is a colorful character. At 73, he still works 14 hour days, six days a week. He raised 8 kids (7 boys and a girl), and now has 14 grandkids. He's been married to my mother for 50 years.

He bought his first business before he was 25, which he recently sold, and has owned his second business for 35 years. He started his working career as a carpenter. (His middle name is Jesus, I'm not kidding.) He rebuilt a 1968 Ford Shelby Mustang in his garage and had a stint as a professional singer (in both English and Spanish). He survived a quintuple bypass heart operation. I've heard him listen to music ranging from Billy Idol to Rimsky-Korsakov. He has a garden of which he is very proud of as well as a fish pond that he spends an inordinate amount of time trying to keep clean.

Clearly, he's learned a few things, some of which he's taught me and some of which I picked up by watching and listening to him. In honor of Father's Day, here are a few things I learned from my father, who we affectionately refer to as "Pops":

Work

Don't make the job more important than the reason for doing it.

If you need to get the job done, sometimes you need to stay up all night to do it.

If you enjoy doing the job, you won't mind staying up all night.

Don't do a half-assed job, do it right so you can take pride in it.

You need to have a good balance of working with both your hands and your head.

Don't be afraid to get your hands dirty.

Favorite saying: "Get it done or I will cloud up and rain all over you."

Lifestyle

Keep a clean house, don't be a slob.

Put if back where you got it from. (There's a place for everything and everything in its place.)

Take good care of your stuff and it will last you a long time.

Don't walk around barefoot if you have toenails that look like claws. Cut the damn things.

People will show you more respect if you dress well.

Life's too short to wear uncomfortable clothing.

You don't need a bunch of fancy products to wash your car; all you need is a hose and a towel. Also, it helps to have kids to do it for you.

Listen to music every day. Don't listen to it too loud or you'll lose your hearing. Once in a while is ok, though.

Learn how to tell a joke and know a lot of good ones. A sense of humor is essential.

So is an occasional stiff drink.

Favorite saying: "Be careful."

Children

Trust that your child will come into the world with a loaf of bread under its arm.

Teach them manners and to be respectful. It's a reflection on you.

You gotta keep your kids busy.

Kids don't need to get everything they want.

Having kids is what you have to go through to get grandkids.

Sometimes you have to forgive or apologize even if you don't want to. Don't let pride get in the way.

Family is very important.

Favorite saying: "I've forgotten more than you'll ever know."

Dealing with People

Most of the time you can get people to do what you want by being pleasant, saying please, and winning them over with a smile.

Sometimes, though, you have to yell really loud to get people moving.

Many people are looking for someone to teach and guide them.

When you meet a person, look them in the eye and shake their hand. Show good manners.

Favorite saying: "Do you see milk dribbling out of the side of my mouth?"

Life's Challenges

Don't let yourself get defeated by a problem. Ask yourself "How can I solve this problem?" There is always a solution. Get really good at solving problems.

Use your imagination to deal with problems. Look around and ask yourself, "What resources are available to me that I can use to solve this quickly?" It might be some tape, a stick, some wire or it might be someone you can call.

Sometimes, when your back is up against the wall, you must get mean.

Prayer. Have faith that God will see you through.

Favorite saying: You don't want people to say about you "He couldn't fight his way out of wet paper bag."

Good Advice

Don't take any wooden nickels.

There are a lot of people walking around with their thumb up their butt and their finger in their ear. Don't be one of those people.

Pay attention!!

Favorite saying: "The angle of the dangle is equal to the heat of the ..." on second thought, let's skip this one.

Don't let 'em get to you.

Thanks Dad, and Happy Fathers Day to all Dads out there.

Favorite saying: "I've forgotten more than you'll ever know."

"Movement = energy."

How to Have Lots of Energy

I'll never forget the time that I found instant energy. For a while I'd been trying to find the energy to get started on all the things I wanted to do. I'd be sitting in front of the television thinking "If only I could find the energy to get off this couch, my life would be a lot better." I felt depressed and unmotivated.

One day while watching Family Guy and eating Captain Crunch, someone knocked at my door. Too tired to get up, I shouted "Come in!" The UPS guy ran in with a package and dropped it right in my lap.

I was too tired to get up and a get a knife, so during the commercial breaks I used my spoon to saw through the tape and open the package. I pulled out the packing peanuts to uncover a strange glow wrapped up in some paper. **I unwrapped the paper and to my surprise, it was some Energy!** I finally had me some!

I jumped right up and cleaned the house. Then I wrote up my resume and went out and found my dream job. The money started rolling in. I started working out regularly, got real buff, and started dating a model. I learned to play guitar and joined a band. We made a record and went on a whirlwind European tour that included fine dining at the fanciest...

I awoke to the opening tune of SpongeBob SquarePants. My bowl of Captain Crunch was all over my lap. **It was just a dream.** "God, I'm tired" I said. The minute I said that my eyes got real droopy. I thought about taking a nap right then and there but the thought of the Captain Crunch all dried and crumbly on my pants was more than I could bear. I jumped up and shouted "NO!" I'm 35 years old! When is my life going to start?"

Then I noticed something interesting. **Just standing up and shouting had given me some energy!** I found some paper and a crayon and wrote down my discovery: *"Movement = energy."*

I realized something else: the minute I said "I'm tired", I felt tired! I wrote down this realization as well. *"Whatever I say, my mind will obey. Energetic language = energy."*

I have a confession. This was not the first time I had fallen asleep while eating sugary cereal. One time I awoke on the couch to find my mouth open with unchewed Cocoa Puffs. I swear I thought I saw a fly flying away. It seems every time I eat a lot of sugar I get sleepy. I got a pencil and wrote this down: *"Good nutrition = good energy."*

I was feeling a bit motivated now. I felt the stirring of energy inside me. I decided to make a list of some things I would do with my bit of energy:

- ✓ Change pants
- ✓ Take all 12 cereal bowls off the coffee table and put them in sink.
- ✓ Wash dishes while listening to Rush's *"Moving Pictures"* really loud
- ✓ Sort through three week-old pile of mail

Now I had some direction, some things I wanted to do.
Curiously, this gave me even more energy. I had another insight and wrote this down: *"Having a plan = energy."*

I was sorting through my mail when I came across a letter from the landlord. *"Ted, you are a month late on the rent. If you don't pay the rent by this Friday I will evict you. Signed, Your Landlord. (p.s. Judging by the overflowing garbage cans in your yard you obviously have enough money for a wide variety of cold cereal, cookies, and pastries. Suggestion: get a life.)"*

The nerve! I was annoyed but also majorly freaked out. Eviction! How could I pay the rent on time if Wendy's wouldn't give me a raise? **I would have to find a better paying job and fast.** I took the abandoned bird's nest out of the spokes of my bike and rode down to the mall and collected a bunch of applications. When I got home, I wrote this down: *"Purpose = energy"*

I filled out a bunch of applications to drop off the next morning. It had been a busy day so I was feeling stressed out and tired. I wanted to sit in front of the tube. **I played my guitar instead and that**

energized me. I practiced *"Blackbird"* for awhile. I felt relaxed and calm now. Before I went to bed at 10:30 I wrote down two things: *"Fun = energy"* and *"De-stress = energy"*

The next day I woke up at 6:30. I felt refreshed. I scribbled *"Good Sleep = Good Energy"*. Out of habit I turned on the news: The Economy. The War. Terrorists. Floods. Car Accidents. I turned off the television, unplugged it and stomped on the remote. It occurred to me that compared to most of the world, I had a pretty good life. I was healthy, I had a place to live, lots of expensive cold cereal, and I had opportunity and the freedom to take advantage of it if I chose to. There was nobody bombing my house or my city. **I felt blessed and was moved by this feeling.** I wrote down *"Gratitude = energy"*.

I eventually took all my insights and made a sign that I hung on my wall:

"I Am Energetic"

- ❖ I have abundant energy because I move my body by walking daily.
- ❖ I have abundant energy because I say that I do. I refuse to say the opposite.
- ❖ I have abundant energy because I have an energy producing diet.
- ❖ I have abundant energy because I have a plan.
- ❖ I have abundant energy because I have a purpose.
- ❖ I have abundant energy because I have a good balance of work, play and relaxation.
- ❖ I have abundant energy because I manage my stress.
- ❖ I have abundant energy because I get enough sleep.
- ❖ I have abundant energy because I focus on what is right with my life and I am grateful.

I started reading this every morning out loud because it energized me.

Here's the key: nothing can give you energy. YOU MUST LEARN TO GENERATE IT. Today, at 50, I'm grateful that I have more energy than I've ever had. I've found a sleep schedule that works for me (11-6). I try to walk every morning. Two days a week I'm a stay home dad with my two daughters, so I work 12-16 hour days four days a week and a few hours early on Sunday writing this blog.

I'm a little busier than I like (we both have huge families that we visit often), but I admit it's my choice. I'm very conscious of how valuable time is. I have a purpose, a plan, and written down goals. I rarely watch television. And I never, ever say I'm tired unless I'm ready to go to bed. There have been a couple of health issues recently that lowered my energy, but I got my butt to my doctor, my chiropractor, and my acupuncturist, and got it back. While writing this, my wife, who had no idea of this week's blog topic, came into my office and said "I've figured out that having energy is mostly in your mind". You can say that again sweetheart!

(Disclaimer: With the exception of the last paragraph, the preceding story is for educational purposes only and is mostly a work of fiction. To the best of my recollection, I have never fallen asleep with unchewed breakfast cereal of any brand in my mouth. However, I did once have to remove a bird's nest from the spokes of my bike.)

Family Guy is an American animated television series created by Seth MacFarlane for the Fox Broadcasting Company.

SpongeBob SquarePants is an American animated television series, created by marine biologist and animator Stephen Hillenburg and distributed by MTV Networks.

"Blackbird" from the album *The Beatles* (1968) by The Beatles, Apple Records.

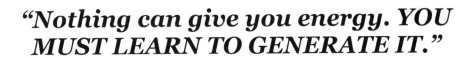

"Nothing can give you energy. YOU MUST LEARN TO GENERATE IT."

"Connect with your inner sense of wonder and creativity and get inspired."

Thirteen Ways to Break Up the Humdrum and Feel Alive

Ever get the feeling that all you do is work and be responsible? Do the days seem to run into each other because the same thing happens day in and day out? Do you feel "stuck"? Henry David Thoreau said *"Most people lead lives of quiet desperation and go to the grave with the song still in them."* Do you sometimes feel that Thoreau is talking about you? (Note: you would be saddened and shocked by the number of people that would say yes to that question.)

It's easy to get caught up in the day to day humdrum. When you ask people how they are doing, how often do you get "Same s..t, different day?"

If you can relate to what I'm talking about, then you need to change some things up. You need to do something different. Here are some tips to bring more joy, aliveness and passion into your life. It all starts with connecting with those things that fill you up inside. The great thing about it is that they are relatively simple things. Seems to be all about the simple stuff, doesn't it?

Listen to music. Music is healing. Music speaks to our souls. Turn off the TV, and sit instead with your eyes closed listening to your favorite type of music. When was the last time you did that? Make a compilation CD of your favorite songs and listen to them in your car instead of listening to the news. I love classical music, and when I'm feeling dulled by life, I listen to Beethoven's *Pastoral Symphony* or Bach's *Sonatas and Partitas for Solo Violin*.

Play music or sing. Do you have a dusty instrument lying around? Pull it out and see if you can become friends again. Could be as simple as a wooden flute with holes or as complex as a grand piano. Have you always wanted to learn an instrument? When would now be the best time to start? Guitar is easy and cheap.

Watch your all time favorite movie. Turn of the phone, grab your favorite brew and be taken away. My favorites: "Lawrence of Arabia" and "Casablanca".

Read. Something that keeps you turning the pages. Something inspiring and interesting. Make regular time to savor it. If you learn something, that's a bonus.

Do some art. Let your artistic side come out. Do you like to draw? Paint? Photography? Work with clay? I don't know how much a bag of sculpey is but I'm sure it's not a lot. You don't need to know "how". Just play, see what happens.

Dance. If you find yourself alone and the mood strikes you then get up and bust a move. Don't be shy to dance alone. It's all about freedom of expression. If you want to but can't call me and I'll help you bust loose. I dance. Usually by myself. Sometimes in front of kids and my wife. This morning I heard someone say they were so happy with their printer that they danced a jig. Cool. That's my favorite "by myself" dance.

Start a garden. Plant a seed. Nurture it. Watch it grow. Maybe you end up with fruit, vegetables or a pretty flower. Be a partner in the miracle of life. Get filled up with wonder. That will make you wonderful (or more wonderful than you already are).

Get a pet. Dogs, cats, birds, whatever. Play with your pet if you have one. Not just walk them. No room or too much hassle? Get a fish. They're easy and they don't mess up your house. Mine just died. I had him for almost three years. We had a ceremony and buried him under the plumeria. Aquariums are peaceful. Get some frogs, or newts. Some people like snakes and lizards. They're not for me but whatever floats your boat.

Get out into nature. Very powerful. Go to a park and walk barefoot in the grass. Take a drive up into the mountains. Take a hike. I like lakes and streams, there's magic in those places. My personal local favorite: Monrovia Canyon Park in Monrovia, CA. Once inside the park, take the Sawpit Canyon Fire Road to the Ben Overturf Trail. Stop and hang out where it crosses the stream. I once saw hundreds of California Newts there after a rain.

Go to a museum. Want to get inspired? Stand in front of a painting that is 500 years old. It's quiet and cool in museums. My favorite: Huntington Library and Botanical Gardens in San Marino. Check out the Japanese Garden or Chinese Garden.

Build something. Anything. A shed. A box. A model airplane. A real airplane.

Take a vacation. Yeah, I know. They disrupt my routine too. Can't afford it? You can't afford not to.

Develop a spiritual practice. Whatever is meaningful to you.

It's all about connecting with your inner sense of wonder and creativity and getting inspired. We are creative beings and when deprived of these essential qualities we shrivel and die, perhaps not a physical death, but certainly a spiritual one. It's up to you to give yourself what you need to thrive.

Casablanca (1942) Distributor: Warner Bros.

"It's not the having or doing that matters. It's the Being."

You've Got It Backwards! It's BE, DO, HAVE

Have you ever heard anybody say "If only I can have this (car, house, relationship, etc...), then I'll be (happy, successful, fulfilled etc.)". Sadly, it seems that all too often people get stuck in "If only..."

That's because it's not the having or doing that matters. It's the Being.

Question: Who are you *Being* now? Are you *being* relaxed? If you are, then you are *doing* something very different than if you were being tense or nervous. That's because *doing* comes out of *Being*. However, many of us believe that if we just *have* the right thing, we will *do* what we want and *be* successful, happy, fulfilled, peaceful, etc. In my experience, though, that's backwards, yet it's the formula that most people follow, and it's called

HAVE DO BE

(If I have this, I will be able to do that, and I will be what I want to be.)

You've Got It Backwards! It's BE, DO, HAVE.

Let me ask you another question. **Who do you think you are?** (Hint: Who do you say you are?) *Who you say you are* is who you declare yourself to be. *What you say you* are is probably going to reflect what you do.

Listen to your own language. Do you say you are happy? Or miserable? Do you say you are competent? Or a loser? Do you say you are lucky? Or cursed? You are what you say you are and what you declare yourself to be.

Listen to other people's language. How often do you hear "I am tired" or "I am sick of this" or "I hate that" (I am hating). Compare what their experience of life is to those who say things such as "I am grateful" or "I'm cool" or "I'm fantastic" or "I'm so good I wish I were twins!".

Some might say, "Oh, they can say that because they have a good job, good marriage, or good luck." But consider, just consider, that they have those good things because of who they declare themselves to Be. Maybe *they* understand that the universe works like this:

BE DO HAVE

(If I am who I want to Be, then I'll do what that type of person does, and then I'll have what that type of person has.)

I didn't come up with this. I learned it in the Landmark Forum, read it in *"Conversations with God,"* * then had it reinforced by T. Harv Eker. It's how the Law of Attraction works.

Let's examine this statement: "If I *have* the perfect job, then I'll make lots of money (*do*), then I will *be* successful." The underlying assumption is "I am not yet successful."

Now try this: "I am successful (Being). I do the things successful people do, and I have the things successful people have." It starts with a declaration of Being. EVERYTHING starts with BEING.

You must declare yourself to BE what you want to BE, then DO the things that that person would do, then you will have the things that that person would have.

It can't be that simple can it? Well yes, but it's not easy! Let's say I declare that who I am is happy. This is a state of being. Does happiness start with what you do? Absolutely not! It starts with an idea, a thought, and a happy mind set. If declare myself to be happy, then I make the choice to be happy, so I now I do the things that happy people do. Like, for instance, smile. What is it about these happy people that they are always smiling?? What is up with that? Are they smiling because they are happy or are they happy because they are smiling? *Does it matter?!* They have a happy life! **If I want a happy life, then I'm just going to have to do what those happy people are doing.**

What do happy people do? My advice is this: find someone who you know is happy and ask them; they won't mind telling you because that's what those darn happy people do, they seem to like to spread their happiness around, can you imagine that? Who do these people think they are?

Um....happy? Duh!

I stood up one day in 2000 and declared to the world (or at least a small segment of the world) *"Who I am is transformation."* I wanted to change my life. I didn't know what the heck transformation involved but it sounded good. (This was before I became a hypnotherapist.) So I started talking like a transformed person. Acting like a transformed person. Hanging out with people who wanted transformation. Reading books about transformation.

Now, I am Transformation Man! Don't sell me on your shortcomings, I won't be convinced! I'm a stand for your greatness, do you get that? Why? Because that is who I declare myself to be, and when I stand in the place of transformation, I am powerful. It doesn't matter that sometimes I feel weak because how I feel has nothing to do with the commitment I have made - to choose powerfully to walk the path of my own personal evolution.

Let me ask you one more question. ***WHO DO YOU WANT TO BE?*** Scarlett O 'Hara declared "As God is my witness, I will never go hungry again!" as she held up a wimpy carrot, but that didn't matter. In that moment, she BEcame something other than just hungry.

If you are not who you want to be, then you must do the same. Declare who you want to be as who you are *now*. Say it out loud, declare it to the universe, tell who ever will listen, write it down, and make it your commitment, your life's purpose, your reason for being here. Scream it from the highest mountain; repeat it a thousand times a day. Then DO. Whenever, however, as much as you can, as often as you can. Ask for help. You'll be stopped, challenged, maybe even ridiculed. Just keep declaring who you are, this is your spirit, this is your essence, this is your energy, and this is your life for God's sake!

Don't waste another moment wishing, hoping or waiting for the right conditions to be who you want to be. Declare yourself to be it now, and declare it with power and conviction. Then do something. And see what happens.

*Walsch, Donald Neale *Conversations with God*. 1996 Putnam Adult

For more information about T. Harv Eker, visit www.harveker.com

---

"It's said the talk is cheap but the truth is that people cheapen talk."

Your Word Can Move Mountains: Five Steps to Integrity

One recent hot weekend my family and I were checking out the pond at the Santa Anita Botanical Gardens. My youngest daughter, The Rock, started to insist "I want to go swimming!" Back in the car, she became even more insistent. We were on our way to my parents' house, so I told her "I give you my word that we'll go swimming in the pool at Grandma's house."

Within minutes of arriving at my parent's house, The Rock and Chick (my older daughter) had their swim suits on and were jumping up and down with excitement. "Can we go swimming?" "In a minute", I said. I didn't feel like going back into the sun. I'd already sat down, cracked a cold one, and was feeling cool and comfortable. Soon they were playing with their cousins as if they had forgotten about the pool. For a second I considered telling them that it was too late to go swimming but instead I jumped up and took them out into the pool. I had given them my word. **How can I teach them integrity if I can't stick to my word?**

It's said the talk is cheap but the truth is that people cheapen talk. Consider that if you regularly cheapen your talk, then you cheapen the quality of your life.

We all know people who "are all talk". When they say they are going to do something, we pay no attention, because they always say things but don't deliver. On the other hand, we know people whose word is their bond. They say "I'll be there at ten o'clock" and we know that come hell or high water they'll be there because that's how that person always is. **We can say that person has integrity.**

According to Wikipedia*:

The word "integrity" stems from the Latin adjective integer (whole, complete). In this context, integrity is the inner sense of "wholeness" deriving from qualities such as honesty and consistency of character. As such, one may judge that others "have integrity" to the extent that one judges whether they behave according to the values, beliefs and principles they claim to hold.

In other words, integrity is consistency between what one says and what one does.

Words can be incredibly powerful and creative. I've heard it said that there is no reality without language. If that statement is true, and I believe it is, then nothing happens without you first speaking it into existence. In Genesis 1:1 it's written *"In the beginning was the Word, and the Word was with God, and the Word was God."* The Bible goes on to say that God spoke the universe into creation.

In the last chapter I talked about declaring yourself to be who you want to be before the doing and having. In the declaring of who you are, you start to create who you want to be. This is the power of your word.

The power of our word is developed first with ourselves by being in integrity with ourselves. It's easier for us to keep our promises to others than it is for us to keep promises to ourselves. Have you ever made a promise to yourself knowing deep down inside that you probably won't keep it? I know I have. This is deadly, for two reasons: one, we can trick ourselves into believing we have integrity when we don't. Second, what integrity we do have will always depend on what we commit to others. **Truth be told, the most powerful promises we make are those we make to ourselves and keep.**

When we commit to being a person of integrity, then our word starts to become powerful because we consistently do what we way we will do. In time, we come to trust that when we commit to something, it WILL happen. This is called creating your life through your speaking. "This I shall do" becomes not just a promise but the starting point, or genesis of what you will accomplish.

Eventually **we can develop our integrity to the point where if we want to create something, we simply speak our intention and it begins to manifest it in physical reality.** We know it will come to pass because we have created our word as powerful. Others know it as well. Our reputation becomes such: "If he said it was going to happen, then you better count on it happening."

At this point, the speaking of something and the creating of it become one. We then have a clear sense of our own personal power and a deep belief in our ability to create whatever we want to create.

Here are five steps to developing the power of your word and creating yourself as someone with unshakable integrity.

Start small. Commit to something you are going to do daily. Keep it simple. It could be reading for 5 minutes or sweeping the floor. Calling your mother, anything. Try to do it for 21 days. If you really want to put yourself out there, commit to doing it at a particular time. The point is to get in the habit of doing what you say you are going to do.

Clean up where you are out of integrity with yourself. Again, start with something small. Maybe you promised yourself you were going to work out three times a week but have yet to start. Simply acknowledge that you are out of integrity with yourself without shame or blame then recommit to something that you CAN do, that is realistic. Maybe one time a week. Or, choose consciously NOT to work out. Maybe it's not something you are truly committed to and that's ok. Be complete with it.

Clean up where you are out of integrity with others. This might be tough but it's essential. What have you promised to someone that you haven't completed? This might involve an apology, re-negotiation, or fulfilling the promise. Leaving these things dangling can be a heavy burden on your mind.

Declare that you are going to do something big and audacious. You don't need to know how you're going to do it, just commit. Make yourself accountable to someone. It's gotta be big! Does this then see what happens...

Realize and accept that you will fall out of integrity. You will break your word. It's what humans do. Don't make it mean anything. Re-commit, re-negotiate, clean it up, and move on.

If your talk is so cheap that even your dog rolls his eyes when you speak, then you need help from the TMan. (Me)

*If you haven't discovered the online fountain of knowledge that is Wikipedia, you should check it out: www.wikipedia.com.

"Life is meaningful, profound, and precisely because it will be done too soon."

The Flash of Light That is My Life

I was having a conversation with two colleagues recently about how quickly time passes. One said that he still felt like a kid inside. The other said, "We all feel that way, yet, when I think about being 60, I realize that I'm nearer to the end of my life than the beginning."

I figure I'm about halfway, at 50 years old. That was fast.

The day before, my daughter started her second week of kindergarten. It was the first chilly day after temps of 100+ here in So Cal. As I walked through the schoolyard with my daughter, there were sights and sounds I've not experienced for many years: children in line, backpacks, classrooms. I still remember my first day of first grade. Has it been 45 years? My daughter's in school now, how did that happen so quickly? Is summer over already? Everything is happening so quickly...

I was camping out on Lake Mohave on the Colorado River last weekend with my brothers and brother-in-law. The first night on the lake we were treated to an incredible lightning storm. We were surrounded on every inch of the horizon by constant lightning flashes, continuously lighting up the pitch black night. It was incredible; something I've seen only a handful of times and only while living in Arizona.

Today, my first day back at work, I drove from my 7 am business meeting to my office, but I didn't stop; I drove right by. I wasn't ready to go in there, sit down, and be contained within four walls. I drove aimlessly for a while, listening to Elvis Costello sing "Poor Fractured Atlas."

I ended up sitting at an outdoor table at a café. I sit there now, the air is cool, and it's still and quiet. The sun shining on me feels good. There are lots of trees and flowers. There's a nursery next door;

when I'm ready to leave I will walk slowly through it, to be close to the green and living things.

Coming back from a few days at the lake is always tough for me. My mind is slow, and I find myself resisting the transition back to "regular" busy life. I want another hour to sit, to watch, to think, to feel my life happen. I'm just not ready to go back to work yet, just give me another hour. There will always be work to do, and life will continue to fly by. For now, I'm standing outside the stream of my life, where I can drink with intention and clarity.

As if in confirmation, a bell rings at the train station, its message: "Train coming, better get on board." A dragonfly flys by me. The last one I saw was at the lake, two days ago as I sat peacefully looking out over the water and reflecting on my life. It seemed to remind me "Don't let it go..."

Life is precious and short. To stay on board with your own life you've got to pay attention, or you'll miss what matters, as it goes by quickly. While sitting in your seat on the ride of your life, you've got to look out the window and be present to your own life as it passes by; the valleys, the peaks, the plateaus, the darkness, the light.

There is a Japanese folk song I like called Sakura Sakura (Cherry Blossoms). To the Japanese, the fleeting beauty of the cherry blossoms symbolizes the brevity of life and the frailty of existence. Like the life of a man or woman, the petals are brief, colorful, and bright for the short duration of their life before they wither and die.

Life is meaningful, profound, and precious precisely because it will be done too soon, and I find myself very present to that now. I can't help but ponder the Big Question: Why are we here, just to be gone in a flash?

I think about that lightning storm. *Maybe it's all about the light.* It's said that everything living is light bound into matter. What if the most profound legacy we can leave, in the short flash of a spark that is a person's life, is the *light* that we bring to the darkness? Those that we revere through history, whose lives and teachings we honor in church and temple, in music and art, were all bringers of light. That light gives us hope, guidance and comfort as we continue along on our journey that is this life.

I think the biggest problem that humans face, and the biggest obstacle to our peace and happiness is that we are blind to our own light. We fail to see it because we're not taught to, or shown how. So how can we see the light in others?

If I can be present to this brief and singular burst of color that is my life, if I can know myself as this lightning flash bound into matter, then maybe I can know your light. And if you can't see it, then maybe I can help you see it. Should I find myself in darkness, maybe you can help me find mine.

After I'm gone, I don't want my kids to remember me for how hard I worked, how much money I made, or how much respect I got. I want them to remember that I helped them know and honor their own light, because I was in touch with mine. I want to light the way for them.

And so I go back to work, back to the busy, but now with a bit more peace. The reason I'm here is to know my light, and then shine it, wherever, whenever, and however I can, into the face of the pitch black of our own blindness. *May we all light the way for each other.*

"Poor Fractured Atlas" from the album *All This Useless Beauty* (1996) by Elvis Costello, Warner Bros., Rhino

"Is your story moving you forward or keeping you stuck?"

Time to Get Rid of Your (Same Old) Story?

My life changed in 1990 when a relationship I was in fell apart like a castle made of sand. Parents had been met and plans made for the future, even though we had only been together less than four months. Perhaps you can relate to the feelings of devastation, shock, and loss that accompany the sudden end of something into which much emotion has been invested. It brought me to my knees.

At the time, I told myself "This is the worst thing that has ever happened to me; this is the worst pain I've ever experienced." My disappointment and resentment consumed me, and at times, my anger bordered on hatred. For a while **this was my story**, and I would tell it to anyone who cared to hear: "I've been terribly, terribly wronged."

This upheaval caused me to look deep inside of me to find out why I was so affected by this short but volatile relationship. What I saw was that there were wounded parts of me that needed healing. I began reading, journaling and working hard to build my self- value and self esteem. I came to realize that I would never have a healthy relationship until I had one with myself. Within a few short years, I had developed a new level of self respect and self acceptance. **I started to tell a new story about what happened.**

Today, 20 years later, I consider that experience to be the greatest gift ever given to me, next to my wife and kids. In spite of a strong desire to hold on to my anger and resentment (...anybody else ever felt that way?), I couldn't ignore the fact that my pain had been a catalyst to begin my own personal journey of self transformation, and for that, I am immensely grateful. I choose to tell *this* story now, and the telling of it empowers me.

What's your story? Do you have a "same old story" you tell all the time, to yourself and others? What's that story doing for you? Is it moving you forward or keeping you stuck? The good news is that you can change that story and choose to tell a new one anytime you want to.

There are always two parts to anything that occurs to you in life. There's what happened, and then there's your story of what happened. The problem is, it's really easy to get the two confused. We can come to believe that our story about what happened *is* what happened and that becomes our reality. Then we start making decisions based on a story that for the most part, we made up.

Much of my work with my hypnotherapy clients involves helping them identify stories they are telling themselves that are disempowering and downright scary. In other words, keeping these stories alive robs a person of confidence, self esteem and aliveness, while perpetuating fear, doubt and unhappiness. The first question I ask of them is: "Ok, something happened to you, but what you are making that mean, and what is that doing for you?"

That fact is that as humans we are meaning making machines. We will make up stories about what happens to us, we can't help it. That's what gives each life its unique flavor. What that flavor tastes like will depend on the meaning that you assign to what happens to you. *"My business failed, that means I'm a failure"* has a pretty bitter taste. On the other hand *"Because my business failed, I learned something that will help me succeed next time"* is a little more palatable, as well as being infinitely more useful.

I recently saw the film *Invictus*. It's about Nelson Mandela's attempts as president of South Africa to unite a country divided by years of apartheid. After 27 year of imprisonment by the South African government, one might expect that Mandela would want to exact revenge on those that imprisoned him. But instead, the story he told himself during his imprisonment is reflected in the poem **"Invictus"***, which he shares with the captain of the South African rugby team (played by Matt Damon):

Out of the night that covers me,
Black as the pit from pole to pole,
I thank whatever gods may be
For my unconquerable soul.

In the fell clutch of circumstance
I have not winced nor cried aloud.
Under the bludgeonings of chance
My head is bloody, but unbowed.

Beyond this place of wrath and tears
Looms but the Horror of the shade,
And yet the menace of the years
Finds and shall find me unafraid.

It matters not how strait the gate,
How charged with punishments the scroll,
I am the master of my fate:
I am the captain of my soul.

As is widely known, Mandela won international respect for his advocacy of national and international reconciliation and in 1993 was awarded the Nobel Peace Prize, shared with Frederik Willem de Klerk.

Our reality is self-created through the meanings and interpretations we attach to the situations and circumstances of our lives, that is, what we think about them. I don't know how much control we have over things that happen to us, but we have full control over what we think.

Want a better experience of life? Choose to think differently, come up with a better meaning, and tell a new story to yourself and others that is inspiring, and filled with courage and hope. You have that choice, so why not choose it? *After all, it's all made up anyway.*

* **"Invictus"** is a poem by the English poet William Ernest Henley (1849–1903).

The film *Invictus* (2009) Distributor: Warner Bros. Pictures

"To begin the process of transformation, we must remove the mask of who we feel we are and try on a new mask (or identity) that is more in line with who we want to be."

Scaring Away the Dark Side of Change

Do you ever wonder why it's a tradition to wear masks on Halloween? Why we dress up and disguise ourselves as Dracula, ghosts, skeletons, witches and monsters?

The modern holiday of Halloween, although considered by most to be a non-religious holiday, has its roots in both the Celtic celebration of Samhain and the Christian holiday of All Saints Day. Samhain (Old Irish: "the end of summer") celebrated the end of the "lighter half" of the year and the beginning of the "darker half". The name Halloween comes from The Eve of All Hallows, or All Hollows Even, meaning the night before All Hallows (Saints) Day. All Saints Day celebrates those departed who have attained eternal and direct perception of God (known as the beatific vision).

The ancient Celts believed that the veil between this world and the Otherworld became thin on Samhain, allowing both harmful and harmless spirits to pass through into the realm of the living. Good spirits of deceased loved ones were invited in while harmful spirits were scared off by wearing costumes and masks. So there you go.

In my work as a hypnotherapist, I help people to change, and we all know that change is not easy. Change almost always involves going from what is known and comfortable to something unknown and uncomfortable. People come to me when they realize that what is known and comfortable (usually habits of thinking and/or behaving) isn't working for them anymore.

This desire to stick with the familiar and comfortable is incredibly powerful, even if we are able realize that our current way of being is self- destructive, hurts others, or keeps us stuck. Our deepest held beliefs about ourselves often exist in our language, when we say *"I'm not good at that"* or *"I can't do that"*. What needs to happen is that new beliefs must be formed, as well as new language. At some point, you must start to create the new belief by saying *"I can get good at this"* or *"I can do that"*, even if you don't feel that it's true.

We can use ancient traditions as a metaphor to understand the nature of change. To begin the process of transformation, or reinvention of ourselves, we must remove the mask of who we feel we are and try on a new mask (or identity) that is more in line with who we want to be. The new mask will be uncomfortable and foreign, but the wearing of it serves to scare off the spirit of the old behavior which causes us harm by holding us back from connecting with our true power and greatness, or our "good (god) spirit". When we don our new identity, we invite that helpful spirit in.

There will be conflict as we seek to get comfortable with our new idea of who we are. We will be tempted to put the old mask back on, and at times, we will. Yet we must continue to wear the new self perception, getting comfortable with it, making it a part of our life. We remain diligent in not allowing the harmful spirit back into our thinking and behavior.

It's the old adage *"act as if"*, or *"fake it until you make it"*. I've had more than one client ask me in disbelief and skepticism, *"Are you telling me that all I have to do is say that I'm who I want to be and I'll become it?"* I answer "No, but that's a really good place to start, *with your language."* **You put the costume on and act the part.**

Quite often while one is letting go of the old behavior and adopting the new, you'll have to deal with the darker half, or shadow side of yourself, that aspect of yourself that aims to sabotage your best efforts.

You'll be challenged by that darker half, and you'll be tested. You'll think it's too hard and will want to give up. Just ask anyone who's tried to quit smoking or lose a significant amount of weight. They'll tell you, *"It's like there's two parts of me, one that wants health and the other that wants to destroy me."*

The best way to scare off that nasty spirit is to enthusiastically (enthusiasm: en theos, or "the god within") keep pretending to be who you want to be, in your language, in your thoughts and most importantly, in your behavior. You must continue to hold on to your highest value, or your highest vision of who you want to be.

If you can triumph over the darker half, if you can ward of the goblins, spooks and ghosts of your past, and come to believe in body, mind and spirit that your are on your way to achieving a possibility for your life that inspires you, (inspire: "the spirit within") then you will find yourself in touch with the beautiful vision of your own divinity.

How interesting that All Saints Day was originally celebrated on May 13th, in the spring. This date coincided with the ancient feast of Lemuria, where the harmful spirits of the darker half of the year are appeased and exorcised.

As we move into the darker half of the year, we can use this time for introspection to go deep into the dark places of self knowledge. We can acknowledge and accept those masks that need to be discarded, and keep their negative influence away with our new face. All traditions have their origins in the human experience, in our desire to release the old and welcome the new and to be in acceptance and accordance with the seasons of life: that ongoing cycle of birth, growth, death and reinvention.

"Honor what came before and what is no more, taking the legacy of knowledge and wisdom and moving courageously into tomorrow."

Are You Haunted by Ghosts?

Halloween is a big thing around our house. My wife is a Halloween nut, so consequently my two daughters, Chick and The Rock, had been frothing at the mouth about getting dressed up and trick or treating. One was a fairy and the other was Minnie Mouse. We were going to take them trick or treating but didn't because they were having too much fun handing out candy to other trick or treaters.

With all this Halloween Hoopla and stuff on TV, The Chick has been seeing ghosts lately. "Dad, there's a ghost in my room" or "I think there's a ghost outside." Of course, I tell her that there are no such things as ghosts, even though *I know that there are.*

I was watching Larry King interview a couple of guys that have this ghost lab that investigates paranormal occurrences. One of the guys suggested that a ghost is the residual energy of a deceased person that won't go away because there is unfinished business.

Are haunted by the energy of unfinished business? Are you aware of specters from your past that keep you stuck in fear and trepidation? For some people, these demons are very real.

It's said that ghosts, if indeed they do exist, don't know they are dead or don't want to be dead. They try to stay among the living, caught in a nether land of not alive but not dead.

How true that can be for many of us that are haunted by past tragedies, traumas, mistakes, and failures. Did events happen in your life that should stay buried but that you continue to resurrect from the grave of the past? Oftentimes these memories can take possession of us and keep us from moving forward.

Failed businesses, painful relationships, bitter divorces, the loss of a loved one, letting someone down big-time, stupid yet costly mistakes, times when we felt we did not measure up to our ideal self. All can become goblin-like and so scary that we never even try again or make judgments about ourselves which are no longer (perhaps never were) true. So we stay inside, windows shuttered, doors locked, afraid to venture out into possibility.

We all have a tendency to look to the past for information about how to act in the future. But the future does not have to equal the past. What's also true is that we are human, and as such, we will make mistakes, suffer loss, hurt people, and fail, perhaps many times before we get it right. **You are human, are you cool with that?**

I'm no ghostbuster, but I think that to allow these ghosts to rest in peace, you may need to:

- Forgive yourself
- Forgive someone else
- Apologize to someone
- Make it up so someone
- Reconnect with someone
- Write a letter but don't mail it
- See the experience from a different perspective
- Recommit to our ideal self
- Find the wisdom and learning from the experience and move on.
- Change something major in your life (it's said that those ghosts don't like remodeling)

If you need a little technique to release the past, try this:

Close your eyes and get comfortable, taking some deep breaths. When you feel centered and grounded, see, feel or get a sense of the situation, person, or experience you want to release. Imagine cords of light connecting you to this situation, person, etc. See, feel or get a sense of a magic or special knife, sword, or scissors in your hand and begin to cut the cords connecting you. When you are done, reattach the cords back to yourself and imagine the cords of the person or situation reattaching back to it or them. Imagine the situation or person fading away or getting smaller or smaller until they disappear. Imagining a grave where the situation/relationship is buried can be helpful to some people.

This is a good time to talk about letting these ghosts rest in peace; today is Dia de Los Muertos, Day of the Dead. Honor what came before and what is no more, taking the legacy of knowledge and wisdom and moving courageously into tomorrow.

"We are human, and we will make mistakes, suffer loss, hurt people, and fail, perhaps many times before we get it right."

"When you're a Zombie you're walking around but you're asleep, dead to anything other than your incessant mind chatter."

Zombies! How to Keep from Being One of the Walking Dead

It's close to Halloween, and people are already talking about what costume they're going to wear. For a couple of days there will be lots of ghosts and skeletons, goblins and witches, vampires walking around.

But regardless of what time of year it is, you can always count on there being **Zombies**.

You've seen them out there. In line at the supermarket. In the car beside you on the freeway. Behind the counter at the store. Looking back at you from the mirror. Zombies are everywhere: *The walking dead!*

One day last month I left my house running late for an appointment. I had a number of things on my mind. I was driving along and the next thing I knew, I had rear-ended a very nice Lexus. *My God! I had slipped into a Zombie state!* It took the appearance of a police officer to bring me back from the brink of disaster.

It doesn't take much these days to become Zombified. Not enough sleep, skipping meals, traffic, noise, too much to do and long days on the job can mush your mind until you find yourself aimlessly wandering around chanting "Brains! Where are my brains?"

What is a Zombie? One definition is *"an automaton: someone who acts or responds in a mechanical or apathetic way."* It can be easy to respond to life like an automaton, mindlessly going from activity to activity, lost somewhere in the maze your own thoughts, not present to any wonder or miracles that might be happening right in front of you.

When you're a Zombie you're walking around but you're asleep. You're dead to anything other than your incessant mind chatter. Life becomes boring and routine. (Same as it ever was...) At the end of the day you can't remember anything you actually did, so you Zombie-out in front of the tube to watch Zombie Housewives.

Another definition of zombie is *a human being who is being controlled by someone else by use of black magic.* I can think of a long list of things that might fall under that category: the media, politicians, advertising, consumerism, the hypnosis of the culture. But that ole' black magic can come from inside as well: guilt, obligation, obsession, compulsion, resentment, anger.

We fall prey to this kind of control when we are overwhelmed. Overwhelm means that there's too much stuff going in your head, too many conversations at the same time, too much to think about. Your brain, that God-given instrument of creation, instead becomes focused on obsessing and worrying about bad things that happened in the past or bad things you think might happen in the future.

When we become overwhelmed we go into a trance state. We become suggestible to any and all negativity going on around us or inside of us. So we end up going around in circles, not creating our own life, but letting it be controlled by environment. We can become dulled to life and its magnificence. We might wake up one day and say "Where did it all go? Where have I been?" You may ask yourself "Well, how did I get here?"

One of his students asked the Buddha, "Are you the messiah?"
"No", answered the Buddha.
"Then are you a healer?"
"No", the Buddha replied.
"Then are you a teacher?" the student persisted.
"No, I am not a teacher."
"Then what are you?" asked the student, exasperated.
"I am awake", the Buddha replied.

There is only one thing to do when you find yourself walking around in the Zombie Zone. Wake up! Reclaim your brain. Get present to your life.

Here are some guidelines to finding your way out of Zombieland.

Mornings are really important as they set the tone for the rest of the day. For some folks, every morning is Dawn of the Dead, but here are two things you can do to change that up.

First, throw away that alarm clock with the same old buzzer or beeper. Why do you want to alarm yourself first thing in the morning? And for God's sake, don't start the day with ZNN. (Zombie News Network) Wake yourself up gently with some music or at least something inspirational.

Second, give yourself some time in the morning to just be. If you are prone to Zombification, you need to wake up not just physically but mentally and spiritually as well. Spend a few minutes just sitting, drinking your whatever, feeling your life, and creating your day before you move on to the next thing, which might be some stretching, walking or reading something inspiring.

Extreme Self Care. Eat right, sleep well, get some exercise, ya gotta be strong!

Count yourself out. If you find yourself spacing out, you can break the spell by saying: "12345 Eyes open wide awake!" This will pull you out of the Zombie trance.

Change your physical position. If you're sitting and you find yourself going into the Zen of Zombie, stand up and walk around. If you're standing, sit down and take a load off. If you're not moving, walk.

Protect yourself with Mindfullness Moments. Have your cell phone or computer give you a reminder every hour to take a short break, a deep breath, or just a few moments to focus on something other than what you're doing.

Ask yourself "What's happening here? Think, but think about what's right in front of you: *your precious life.*

With the coming of the holidays, especially Halloween, you can be sure there will be plenty of opportunities for the Zombie Zoo. Protect yourself and your brain! Be awake, be aware and pay attention!

"Taking time to be with you can be one of the greatest gifts you can give to yourself because it results in self knowledge."

Are You a Nasty Witch or Freaking Ogre? Take Time for Yourself

Of the all the things that I hear in my office this is the most common: *"One part of me wants this, and another part of me wants that..."* Usually one part is unhappy with the other part because it's not doing what the first part wants it to do, like quit smoking or get more motivated to exercise. Can you relate? I can.

We're all trying to get our wants and needs met, but first we need to be clear about what they are. Otherwise, we can become crabby, irritable, unhappy and downright nasty. That's when people start telling us things like "Wow, you sure are being a nasty witch today!" or "Man, why are you such a freaking ogre today?" Well, maybe not in those exact words. Sometimes we can't even put a finger on why we are irritable or crabby. **That's a sign it's time to give yourself some time to yourself.**

Most of us are a collection of many different wants, needs and desires pulling us in many different directions. If you throw job and family responsibilities into the mix, things can get pretty complicated. It's easy to avoid thinking about something within us that needs attention until we can no longer ignore it. In my opinion, many people have no clue who they are because they've never spent much time with themselves.

Taking time for you and being with yourself can be one of the greatest gifts you can give to yourself because it results in *self knowledge*.

It's a way to honor yourself as well as your wants and needs, and to get clear about what those are. This is not a luxury, it's a necessity.

If you are in a relationship such as marriage, that relationship grows out of time spent with each other. Even if you have kids, an effort needs to be made to nurture that relationship. In the same way, it's necessary to develop a relationship with yourself by spending time doing something you enjoy.

Of course, we all have responsibilities; things we need to do and places we need to be. The idea of taking time to yourself might appear to be impossible, if not downright ridiculous and unnecessary.

Yet, the whole idea of transformation involves moving towards freedom and away from constraint. To be free means you have a choice. A choice as to who you want to be and what you want to do. However, it's easy to get caught up in being who you think you should be according to someone else's standards.

In a previous chapter I talked about how we can become zombies from overwhelm and can become like the walking dead. Never taking time for yourself to do what you enjoy or like to do, can result in irritability, stress, tension and becoming difficult to live with, for yourself as well as others.

I have a wife and kids. These are relationships that need time and attention, lots of it. My relationship with myself also needs time and attention. Most of the time I get along with me but sometimes I don't. Sometimes I'm critical of me or downright mean to me or careless with me. It can get so bad that I end up not liking myself very much. Ever been there?

It's better to be your own best friend. If you're upset with your friend, and that relationship is important, then you'll eventually want to have a conversation with that friend, resolve whatever it is that's coming between you. But first you need to spend time with that friend.

Learn to be comfortable with yourself; learn to enjoy your own company. Not so easy if you're not used to it. The constant need to be with others can become an addiction. It can be a distraction from what ails you deep inside.

Here are some ideas for hanging out with yourself (and being cool with it.)

Take a walk, read a book, go to a park or museum. This is time to rejuvenate and calm your mind. It might mean taking a day off of work.

Journaling is a very powerful way to be with yourself, to get intimate with your thoughts and feelings.

Hypnotherapy is one very effective way to get present to what's going on in your head and in your life. Talking to a friend, priest or counselor is also time you give to yourself to explore your inner life, which is the most important part of your life, because all else is a reflection of that inner life.

Exercise, yoga and mindfulness practices like meditation are other ways.

Take yourself out to dinner. Take a drive just to drive and listen to music.

In our busy world, most people will not do this until crisis occurs, then taking time might be a short stay in the hospital. It doesn't have to come to that. Give yourself what you need on a regular basis and you will notice that not only will people want to spend more time with you, but you'll be happier with yourself. Then you only need to be an ogre or witch at Halloween.

"Sometimes there are parts of us that go dormant through non-use or neglect."

Maybe Everything That Dies, Someday Comes Back

I remember the day I got sent home from a job for being a lousy salesperson. It was 1986 and I had a sales job in Phoenix. I was general manager of the business and I was doing pretty good, although I was working 7 days a week, 12 to 13 hours a day.

I went into a sales slump. All of a sudden I couldn't sell water to a man dying of thirst. The pressure to perform was intense and I was failing. One day I walked into the office with my head down and the boss saw my zombie face. "Get outta here Ted, go home, I don't want your negativity infecting the sales team."

I got into my car dejected, defeated and demoralized. I drove home feeling like stepped-on poop. What was wrong with me? Why couldn't I produce? What if I never sold anything again?

Just at that moment, I drove past a park in Scottsdale with a beautiful lake. Fountains sprung out of the lake into the air. It was a glorious spring day and the mountains reflected off the water. Just at that moment, a great song came on the radio. Something inside me shifted. It was like I woke up.

Suddenly, the job didn't matter. It didn't matter whether I sold anything again or not. I'd get another job if I needed to. What awoke within me was amazement and appreciation for this beautiful world. I had allowed it to go dormant. I went home and listened to some music, something I hadn't done in a long time but really enjoy. I got re-connected with me. The next day I went back to work and started selling again like a machine.

Sometimes there are parts of us that go dormant through non-use or neglect. Wonder, curiosity, amazement, silliness, fun, doing the things we love. These things constitute a connection with who we really are. When we lose touch with who we are, we experience *Koyaanisqatsi,* a Hopi word meaning "crazy life, life in turmoil, life out of balance, life disintegrating, and a state of life that calls for another way of living." Our love for life and our joy in living can get covered up by habits and routine and schedule. But it's love and joy that keep us inspired and fulfilled. I believe that to be really alive is to allow those parts of us to flourish. The alternative is to walk around so caught up in what you *have* to do that you lose sight of what you *want* to do and who you *want* to be.

I pulled weeds all day Sunday. I mean I was on my knees, down and dirty, looking under the bricks to get to those lousy weeds. It's amazing what happen when you start digging around in the dirt. You realize that there is a whole world of creatures living there. Spiders, earthworms, pill-bugs, aphids, ants. I've always found bugs interesting. It never occurred to me that I was sharing my property with so many.

The Rock, my three year old daughter, came up to me with an earthworm in her hand. "Look it's a snake!!" She was very excited. She handed the "snake" over to her older sister, Chick, and started to collect pill-bugs. They ran to the backyard and when I caught up with them, they had created a circle of rocks to corral the earthworm, who by now was looking a little weary of the whole affair. "It's a worm, and if you don't put it back in the dirt it'll get sick and die." They obliged.

As we get into the darker half of the year, things go dormant. The leaves fall and the sun spends more time vacationing down south. We have a tendency to want to sleep more, and stay indoors. Bruce Springsteen sang: *"Everything dies baby, that's a fact. Maybe everything that dies, someday comes back."* * We know that when the sun comes back there will be new life. Will that be same with you?

This time of year is a perfect time to resurrect those valuable parts of you that you have lost touch with. To bring out of dormancy those positive aspects of you that speak to what you are really about.

What did you used to do at one time that made you feel alive and inspired? What did you used to do that awakened wonder, curiosity and amazement? Are you willing to go there again, maybe a little bit differently?

We're all busy. It's good to be busy, productive, making money, accomplishing things. I'm only suggesting that you always ask yourself one question: *"Am I busy growing the best parts of me, or am I busy destroying them?*

*From the song "Atlantic City" from the album *Nebraska* (1982) Columbia

"We are continually called to action, to be great, bold, and courageous."

The Hero's Journey

I have to admit I'm kind of a Star Wars nerd. "The Empire Strikes Back" is probably my all time favorite movie. So when I think about the word transformation, I think about Luke Skywalker, the hero of the first three Star Wars movies.

Here's a guy that goes from being a whiny, irresponsible young farm boy to becoming the powerful Jedi Knight that brings peace to the universe by bringing down the evil Galactic Empire. Only in the movies, right? Well, not quite.

The story of Luke Skywalker is a story as old as time. It is known as the Hero's Journey, and it is found in many tales from myths and legends from around the world. The roots of the hero's journey go back to the ancient wisdom teachings from the earliest of civilizations.

George Lucas, the creator of Star Wars, acknowledges that he owes a debt to mythologist and author Joseph Campbell, whose theories about the hero's journey have influenced many writers and artists.

In his book, "The Hero with a Thousand Faces"* Joseph Campbell uses the term "monomyth" to describe the hero's journey. (Click here for a really cool video regarding the hero's journey and "The Matrix")

According to Wikipedia: "Campbell describes a number of stages or steps along this journey."

The hero starts in the ordinary world, and receives a call to enter an unusual world of strange powers and events (a *call to adventure*).

If the hero accepts the call to enter this strange world, the hero must face tasks and trials (a *road of trials*).

At its most intense, the hero must survive a severe challenge, often with help earned along the journey.

If the hero survives, the hero may achieve a great gift, which often results in the discovery of important self-knowledge.

The hero must then decide whether to return with this gift (the *return to the ordinary world*), often facing challenges on the return journey.

If the hero is successful in returning, the gift may be used to improve the world.

Here's the chart they have at Wikipedia:

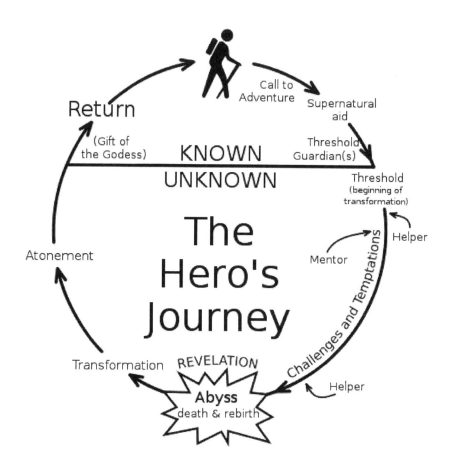

What does this all this have to do with hypnotherapy? Well, I was amazed when I saw this chart, because it looks very similar to another diagram that I am very familiar with:

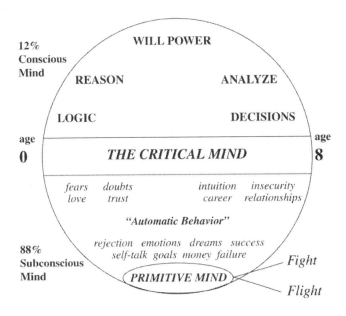

THEORY OF THE MIND

"How Hypnosis and Suggestibility Works"

12%
Conscious
Mind

WILL POWER

REASON   ANALYZE

LOGIC   DECISIONS

age **0**   age **8**

THE CRITICAL MIND

fears   doubts   intuition   insecurity
love   trust   career   relationships

"Automatic Behavior"

88%
Subconscious
Mind

rejection   emotions   dreams   success
self-talk   goals   money   failure

PRIMITIVE MIND

Fight

Flight

Right Brain Suggestibility: The Emotional and creative side that listens literally but speaks inferred.
Left Brain Suggestibility: The logical and detail side listens inferentially but speaks literally.

Coincidence? I think not. Any substantial change or transformation means stepping into the unknown and facing the enemy inside. Let's examine the hero's journey from the perspective of Theory of Mind. The top part of both circles is the ordinary world, the realm of our conscious minds.

As we mature, we are called to adventure. This call is for us to take responsibility for our lives. This may involve going away for school, getting married, starting a career, or having children. This is a call most of us are willing to answer. Of course, there are challenges, sometimes major.

In our journey to create a life, we encounter the road of trials: loss of innocence, loss of love, rejection, disappointment, failure, intense pain, illness. At this point we may be made aware of our own character defects that brought us to this rocky road. These defects can be bad habits or addictions, mental or physical laziness, or values that are lacking, not clearly defined or not adhered to.

At this point there is a threshold to cross. We can choose to play it safe, doing the same thing, stuck in behaviors that don't serve us, stopped by fear of the unknown. Growth and transformation calls, but we may choose to ignore it.

Or, we can choose to delve into the unknown, making a conscious choice to continue along the road of trials in search of a life that is meaningful and worth living, even if the path is unclear. We may realize that we cannot do it alone, and search for guidance in spirituality or religion, seeking out mentors, or being open to help from powers unseen.

Now we are in the abyss, the realm of the subconscious mind. We may have to fight demons that arise to keep us from moving ahead. We might feel helpless and confused as we try to deal with life from a perspective that may be foreign to us. We come face to face with our fears and doubts. Our primitive mind will kick in with fight or flight as a last ditch attempt to protect us from the unknown. We will want to turn back or quit altogether.

If we choose to continue on the path to transformation, *a part of us must die.* Luke Skywalker, in his battle with Death Vader ("Dark Father" representing the evil part of him) loses his hand and throws himself into the abyss, choosing death instead of surrender to the Dark Side. What dies in us is our identification with our ego, who we think we are: our limitations, our physical bodies. We become present to who we really are: infinite energy, light, spirit.

We can now enroll our subconscious minds as a helper, as we work to get comfortable with new ways of thinking, behaving, and relating to ourselves. Our true powers are revealed to us: trust, faith, intuition, courage, self assurance. We have now have acquired the gifts of wisdom and foresight. We've developed clearly defined values that guide us and that are not negotiable.

We are now transformed, born again, and as such, we may seek to share our learning (the gift) to the world as we incorporate and synthesize our wisdom back into ordinary life.

The hero's journey is humanity's struggle to bring order out of chaos. Each of us walks the path of the hero's journey, whether we realize it or not; in our daily lives, we seek transcendence over the mundane, the petty and the ordinary.

We are all continually called to action, to be great, bold, and courageous. We will shy away from this call, yet it is unceasing. Transformation happens when we go boldly where we have not gone before, to quote a phrase, and trust that the universe conspires in our favor.

See yourself as the hero when you feel stuck, beaten, or paralyzed to move forward. You are fighting the same battle that each person fights, travelling the same journey as every human that ever lived. It is the struggle to become more than what we are.

The films *Star Wars Episode IV: A New Hope* (1977) and *The Empire Strikes Back* (1980) Distributor: 20th Century Fox

*Campbell, Joseph *The Hero With a Thousand Faces*. 1949 Pantheon

"Maybe the highest form of gratitude you can have is feeling lucky to be alive."

It's Better to Be Grateful Than Dead

I was originally going to write a post for this week titled "Wake Up or Die". I realized that might be a little harsh for Thanksgiving week and perhaps I should focus on the gratitude thing.

Someone once told me "Ya gotta be alive to be grateful." **There may be some dead that are grateful** aside from Jerry Garcia and the band, but maybe the highest form of gratitude you can have is feeling lucky to be alive.

Why do we only have one day year dedicated to giving thanks? If it was up to me, we would have Thanksgiving Day once a week, (minus the huge feast). Think about it: if you lived 80 years, Thanksgiving Day once a year would give you 80 days when you were reminded to give thanks. If you had it every week, you'd have 4,160 days to make an effort to be grateful. Think that would make a difference in your life? You betcha.

What's so great about being grateful? Well, try going one week without saying thank you or being appreciative for anything. Complain loud and incessantly that whole week. Walk around with a feeling of entitlement, that the world owes you, and see how you feel. Compare and despair while you eye the goodies that others have that you have not.

Gratitude is not just an attitude; it's an energy that you generate. *If you're looking for it,* you might feel it while driving past the San Gabriels, painted in red by the setting sun, or standing outside at night freezing your buns off but awash in the glory of a full moon. It make take some practice generating it until you're feeling moments of bliss on a regular basis, but believe me, it's worth it.

Gratitude is not just something you say or think, it's a feeling that sustains you through the tough times, or gives you the icing when you've got your cake and you're eating it too.

Everything looks better, feels better, works better when you're grateful. Feeling grateful feels good. Feeling good is good for you, physically, emotionally and spiritually. We know that prolonged negative feelings can adversely impact health. And really, feeling thankful as a way of life is not that hard to do.

I spoke with a woman once who had recently lost her husband. She told me that she used to give him a terrible time because of his snoring, banishing him to the couch. "What I would give now to have that sound awaken me just one more time" she said, as she looked down at her wedding ring.

I think about that when the sound of little feet approaching my bed wakes me in the middle of the night. "I'm scared Daddy!" They climb aboard, and it always means less of a sound sleep; they're not aware of whose head gets kicked while they thrash about in a child's sleep. What a small price to pay for the smell of their hair, the sound of their breathing. I know that all too soon I might keep myself awake wondering if they are ok and when they will be home, if I'm lucky to live long enough to see that stage.

Because life is fragile and unpredictable. One second too soon or a minute too late and there's a funeral, or some other tragedy, loss or catastrophe. Anything can be taken from you at any time. I appreciate my grandmothers and grandfathers so much more now that they are gone than I ever did when they were alive. I didn't really appreciate my eyesight until I was brought down by a rare eye disorder. Didn't appreciate the value of money until I found myself without any. Didn't really appreciate my siblings and parents until I was far, far away from them. Maybe you need to go through some tough times to really appreciate the blessings that have been bestowed upon you. Don't wait for that to happen, is my advice.

Every time I see a person sitting at a bus stop in the freezing cold or blazing heat, I'm thankful I have a car. With air conditioning and a heater. I know what it's like to be cold, hungry, lonely and broke, so now that I'm warm, well fed, surrounded by three beautiful females in my own home, and able to buy ice cream whenever I want to, I'm feeling most of the time like life is grand. On top of that, I have work that is meaningful. Remember that icing I was telling you about?

To be alive means you *can* be grateful. You get to have that chance. For your sake, take it. You've been given the fertile ground to plant and harvest the seeds of gratitude before that ground becomes your bed. Be thankful. *For every single little thing.*

"Everything looks better, feels better, works better when you're grateful. Feeling grateful feels good."

"Humans have been dealing with feelings of social alienation, loneliness, and detachment since societies were created."

Do Space Aliens Feel Alienated?

I was standing in my back yard one night looking up at the Orion Constellation. It was cold and quiet. Suddenly, without any warning, I was blasted with an intensely blinding light, causing me to shut my eyes and fall to the ground!

The light quickly diminished, and when I was able to open my eyes, I found myself not in my backyard anymore, but in a circular steel room filled with a strange light. With a gasp, my bones went cold as I realized that I had been **abducted by aliens!**

An invisible door slid open and a tiny alien, not more than a foot high, shuffled toward me. He looked just like those aliens you see in the movies with the really big eyes, except he was wearing a Star Wars T Shirt.

"Not in Kansas anymore, are ya bud?" For such a tiny fellow, his voice was a cross between James Earl Jones and Matthew McConaughey. A plush chair appeared from nowhere and he sat down. I thought about stepping on him, but he must've picked that up because he said "I can vaporize you with a thought, so sit down." I sat on the plastic folding chair that materialized behind me.

"You're some kind of therapist, right?" he said with a heavy sigh.

"I-I-I'm a hypnotherapist, I stammered, "but I..."

"Then can ya shut up and listen? It's not all about you pal." He sounded tired and defeated. "I feel like I'm not a part of anything these days. I just don't know my place in the universe." I don't feel any connection to anything. I feel..."

"Alienated?" I offered.

"Yeah, alienated, smart ass. You probably have no clue what I'm talking about. Why did I decide to come to planet Knucklehead? I should've looked for someone on Cygnus x-1!" He looked so sad, I felt the urge to pick him up and hug him.

"Touch me and I'll have you probed, punk!" now sounding like a cross between Darth Vader and Clint Eastwood.

"Okay, calm down," I replied. "Look, I do have a clue. In our culture, **alienation is a big problem.** Especially this time of year."

"The silly season?"

"There are people who call it that. **Some humans feel alienated and disconnected this time of year because they don't feel a part of everything that's going on.** They look around and see others getting together with family, enjoying traditions, or spending lots of money, and it makes them feel left out if they don't have those things, or they just feel overwhelmed."

"We don't have families. We're raised on pod farms." he said flatly.

"Bummer," I said.

"Yeah, real bummer. I travel this vast universe, from galaxy to distant galaxy, so much space, so little life. Chunks of floating dust balls, gas clouds, stars being born, dying. What does it have to do with me? I'm a speck. **All this technology, all this science, still doesn't keep me from feeling alone, apart, and like there is no meaning to it all.**"

"Kind of like that old song 'Rocket Man.'"

"Yeah, but this ain't no rocket, chump. This space ride has a state of the art plasma drive that will get you from 0 to nowhere in the blink of your primitive eye. And don't forget it, fossil fool."

"Just relax there, big guy. Point is that we humans have been dealing with feelings of social alienation, loneliness, and detachment since societies were created, particularly in our modern age. Our philosophers from Karl Marx through Kierkegaard and Heidegger and even Pope John Paul II have dealt with this issue.

"You seem knowledgeable, human."

"Nah, I'm just good with Wikipedia. Consider this: if you're looking for meaning, you may never find it. Like you said, it's a big cold universe out there. Dust balls and nebulae probably don't mean anything by themselves. But you are a part of the universe that can think, and you can make it mean something, like beauty or order or intelligence. You're like humans in that...

"Careful! Don't compare me to a species that just came down from the trees!!

"Sorry. As intelligent beings, humans have in common the need to make meaning. But I don't think there's any meaning aside from the meaning we choose to create. Which is good, because then we can make things mean whatever we want them to, as long as it supports us in being who we want to be. Of course, who you want to be is also determined by you."

"Hmm," he said pensively, rubbing his little alien chin.

"Once you decide on a meaning that resonates with you, then you can connect with other people, or, uh, beings, that feel the way you do. Then you're a part of something and not so, you know, um, alienated. I'm sure you have friends?"

"I'm in touch with some of my pod mates."

"Okay, so why not develop a better relationship with them, then maybe they can become your family. I read something once: 'The bond that links your true family is not one of blood, but of respect and joy in each other's life. Rarely do members of one family grow up under the same roof.'"*

"Interesting. Continue."

"So you can make your life mean whatever you want, whatever floats your ship. You can create connection with whoever you choose, or contribute to whomever or whatever you choose. There was a time when I felt alienated at the holidays, when I was younger and single, until I created my own meaning for them. I've also created my own meaning for my life, why I'm here, and how I should live it. Now that's my meaning, and I own it."

"I see now that I have chosen to isolate myself in the empty darkness surrounding the stars and nebulae."

"So did I at one time. Now I've chosen to be part of a family."

"A female companion and two smaller but very loud females."

"It's called a wife and two kids. How'd you know?"

"I have the ability to transport you to my starship from a distant galaxy but I'm not smart enough to Facebook you?"

"Right. Point is, your family can be anyone who you feel the desire to share a part of yourself with. Look at you and me; we've connected, haven't we?"

"Indeed. You give me things to think about, surprisingly, for a life form obsessed with keeping coffee grounds out of the kitchen sink."

"I'm only human, after all."

"My condolences. Time to zap you back to your dwelling, then I'm outta here. Your culture's holiday music is driving me nuts."

"Wait! How'd you find me? Where'd you get that T-shirt? What's your name?

"Google - Spielberg gave it to me - the name: unpronounceable to you. Translates to "Great Things Come in Small Packages."

"You're pulling my leg."

"I said it, I meant it, and I'm here to represent it. Hasta la vista, baby."

In the next blink, I was in my backyard again, the Orion Constellation staring down at me hard and bright through the crisp night sky.

Beings from the other side of the cosmos feeling disconnected and alone. Guess it's a small universe after all.

*Quote by Richard Bach

"Rocket Man" by Elton John from the album *Honky Chateau* (1972) Uni

"Once you decide on a meaning that resonates with you, then you can connect with other beings that feel the way you do. Then you're a part of something..."

"The most valuable asset you will ever own is your own body."

The Greatest Gift You Will Ever Give to Yourself

Your Most Valuable Asset

What do you value most in your life? Is it your house or car? Your investments? Is it your family? Your job?

It's often suggested that the things we value most are those that we have worked and sacrificed for; those things that do not come easy to us.

I'd like to suggest that your most valuable possession is one you got for free. It was given to you as your birthright as a human being. It is one of the greatest miracles that exist, and one of the most complex mechanisms found on the planet. Should you lose this, the game is absolutely over.

The most valuable asset you will ever own is your human body. It is the vehicle that houses your mind and spirit. Powered by an intelligence not completely understood, in almost all cases it develops into the highest form of being walking the earth, able to think, feel and create on a wondrous and seemingly limitless scale.

Yet, for all its complexity, for all its miracle and wonder, and in light of the fact that have much control over how long it travels with us, most of us take it almost completely for granted.

Not only do we take it for granted, most of abuse it. Regularly. Consistently. With our thoughts, with our food, and with our movement, or more accurately, the lack there of.

Yet, its design allows it to heal itself, surprisingly, even from the most catastrophic illness or accident.

Except when it doesn't.

When it doesn't, when its inability to repair itself reaches a critical stage, it calls to us for attention. If we don't pay attention, it calls louder. And if we still refuse to hear, it will bring us down.

At that point, almost everything else that we value falls by the wayside as meaningless, in the face of the struggle to regain our health. We become very aware of the preciousness, as well as the fragility, of our bodies. The only other thing that increases in value is our relationships with the ones we love. Ironically, if we have been negligent, careless, or abusive with our health, they will share in suffering the consequences with you.

My Recent Trip to the ER

I was taking out the trash a few weeks ago and a felt my heart do a few flip flops. This had been happening on and off for a few months, but I didn't think anything of it. This time, however, I put my finger on my pulse and actually felt my heart skip a beat. That got my attention. This was not some digestive thing, it was my heart. Still, I felt OK... but, why I take a chance? My uncle had just recently suffered a heart attack which he fortunately survived.

An hour later I found myself in the emergency room at the hospital where my daughters had been born. All I could think was "I'm in the emergency room and they're monitoring my heart...not good." One of the first things they ask is about your family history. Let's see, grandpa suffered 11 heart attacks including the fatal one. Of his five boys, including my father, the youngest died at 43 from a heart attack while playing basketball, and three have survived heart attacks...to say I was confronted with my own mortality would be putting it lightly.

Long story short, they didn't find anything, including putting me on a treadmill where I lasted longer than most. Aside from a real problem, sometimes the heart experiences irregular beats for various reasons, such as stress or caffeine.

Still, I heard my body loud and clear. Since I've had kids, I still walk, but not daily like I used to. I don't get out hiking much anymore. I find I can't eat whatever I want anymore. I do yoga daily, but I realize that I need to do more to protect my health. At 50 years old, if I don't actively maintain it, it will decline. I have at least another 15 years of raising kids. If it took some time in the ER to realize this and motivate me, then I can only feel grateful.

Give Yourself A Gift

This holiday season and the coming New Year, seriously consider giving yourself the gift of health. It's the greatest gift you will ever give to yourself. Don't wait until the first of the year, or until you're in the ER, or receiving a diagnosis you don't want to hear. When you're healthy, life awaits you, opportunity abounds, and everything is so much easier. When you're not, nothing is good.

If you know that you're neglecting your health, then I challenge you to make a commitment to change. Do what you can. Start small. Get off the couch, and up from the computer. You don't need a gym membership or fancy equipment. Start by taking a walk, doing yoga, riding a bike, or taking a class. It doesn't take much to positively affect how you feel, and what your future will look like. Just a few consistent actions done daily.

It's true that you are what you eat and that most people dig their graves with their teeth. Dietary habits are an indispensable part of staying healthy. Start with going through your pantry and getting rid of the stuff that you know you shouldn't be eating. Focus on eating consciously.

I'm not going make any further recommendations because we all know what to do. If you don't, educate yourself. There are so many different philosophies out there about how and what to eat. Find one that makes sense to you and follow it. So much knowledge out there, and for free! Your life, and the quality of your life, as well as the quality of the life of your loved ones, is literally in your hands.

I'm making a commitment to you that I'm going to start walking every day and I want you to hold me accountable. My goal is to live to be over 100 years old with a good quality of life. I hope that we can hang out sometime in 2060.

"Connecting with that quiet place within will give you the space to plant the seeds of your own transformation."

Season of Darkness, Season of Light

Something happened on December 21st at 3:38 pm, PST. The sun was at its lowest point on the horizon, the point in the year where the night is longest and the day is the shortest in the Northern Hemisphere. This is known as the winter solstice, and many people associate this with pagans, druids and Stonehenge. However, it's a natural, astronomical event that is scientifically calculated to the second.

Humans from ancient times on have observed this natural movement from the dark to the light, and have celebrated it in many different ways. It's symbolic of rebirth and new beginnings, as the sun begins its conquest over the cold and darkness of winter. The days will now get longer and warmer until the summer solstice in June, when the sun's daily path across the sky is at its highest. It then starts moving slowly closer to the horizon to where winter once again re-asserts itself.

Throughout the world there are many celebrations this time of the year because humans recognize that our existence depends on the light of the sun. We celebrate light, for example, with brightly colored lights hung on our houses and trees, and with holiday candles. We gather together to ward off the cold and the darkness.

The most popular celebration is Christmas, celebrating the birth of Christ, believed by Christians to be the Light of the World, and as God's son, bringing the world from darkness to light.

Jews celebrate **Hanukkah,** also known as the Festival of Lights, and the Buddhists celebrate **Bodhi Day** on December 8th, the day the Buddha received enlightenment. **Diwali** is the Hindu Festival of Lights celebrating the victory of good over evil. The list of winter festivals goes on and on.

Light is the universal symbol for the light of spiritual awareness. To me, spiritual awareness is acknowledging and connecting with that part of us which is infinite, and all knowing. (You might call it God, Infinite Intelligence, Higher Consciousness, whatever your belief system...) As a hypnotherapist involved in transformational work, my goal is to help people increase their awareness on all levels, and to shine this light of awareness on those dark, shadow parts of themselves that hold all of us back from realizing our full potential as creative beings.

A popular word this time of year is peace. Amidst the hustle and bustle of the season, can you take time to connect with the peace that lies deep within you? Connecting with that quiet place within will give you the space to plant the seeds of your own transformation. You might do this through quiet reflection, meditation or prayer. Take some time to yourself to think about your life, and how you want it to be.

Don't wait until the New Year to plant those seeds. Begin now to write down goals, dreams and visions of what you want to create for the coming year: happiness, health, strength, confidence, abundance. Think about what's working for you and what needs to be released that may be holding you back. If you need some help focusing, give me a call.

Some people believe that we are seeing a new species of human born now on the earth. Alberto Villoldo, author of "Shaman, Healer, Sage"* refers to this new species as Homo luminous. If this is true, (and I would like to believe that it is) then we are continuing to evolve as humans beings. Let us walk courageously through this dark time, as well as through our own darkness, as we celebrate the light within, in all of our many different ways. The evolution of our human family need not wait for generations, but can happen now, starting with you.

*Villoldo, Alberto *Shaman, Healer, Sage.* 2000 Crown Archetype

"The evolution of our human family need not wait for generations, but can happen now, starting with you."

In Closing...

I hope you enjoyed my book and that you got some inspiration, motivation or at least a few new ideas for creating a life that you can love. The key is to hold the vision of how you want it to be, then start making small changes by doing something every day, whether it's exercising, meditating, reading, working on that project, doing affirmations or writing in a journal. It's not easy, but it can be simple: **just start doing something different and do it daily until it becomes a new habit.**

I invite you to visit my blog, *Ted's Tips for Transformation,* from which these chapters have been taken. You can subscribe so that you get my weekly posts delivered to your email inbox. You can hear interviews I've done, watch videos I've made, and read my latest blog posts. Just go to **www.TedsTipsBlog.com.**

This book comes out of what I've discovered in the course of my career as a hypnotherapist, so on my site you can also read about what I do, how I help my clients, and how I might be able to help you. Check out the next few pages for the "Ultimate Free Gift" from me to you.

In addition, you can follow me on Facebook, Twitter, LinkedIn and You Tube.

I wish you health, happiness, and success in your journey through life. To live a life that is meaningful and worth living is a choice. I invite you to make that choice powerfully.

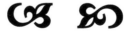

Turn the page for a Free Special Offer only for readers of "The Ultimate Guide to Letting Go of Negativity and Fear and Loving Life"

The Ultimate Free Gift to Help You Start Loving Life Now!

You have the innate ability to change your life starting now! It all starts with getting rid of **"stinkin' thinkin'"** and focusing your mind of **what you want.** It's said that most people are six inches from success: the distance between their ears! If you don't know how to start harnessing the incredible power of your mind, the good news is that you can learn from **Ted A. Moreno, Certified Hypnotherapist and Success Performance Coach.**

Ted is giving you an opportunity to "jump start" your goals by offering you a free *Blueprint for Success Goal Setting Session.* Ted will spend up to 30 minutes helping you get clear about what you really want in your life and will coach you on what steps to take to start realizing your dreams. Whether it's more money, better health, a meaningful career, or fulfilling relationships, you'll find this *Blueprint for Success Goal Setting Session* invaluable. For absolutely no charge* you'll receive:

Blueprint for Success Goal Setting Session. A 30 minute coaching session to guide and motivate you to take action now! You'll have a chance to focus on where you want to be successful in your life and start creating a plan to make it happen. (Value $125)

Your Blueprint for Success: Action Steps. You'll receive a personalized guide detailing steps to take to begin moving toward your stated goals, dreams and desires. (Value 29.99)

Special Thank You Gift Package including Ted's "Peaceful Place" Relaxation CD. As special thanks for reading this book and taking action, you'll receive a special gift package that includes Ted's studio produced relaxation CD *Peaceful Place* featuring 20 minutes of tranquility and relaxation. (Value $44.99)

Total Value   199.98

FREE for readers of this book.

Success is in Your Hands!

To claim your free gift, just email hypnosis@tedmoreno.com with "Ultimate Free Gift" in the subject line along with your contact information, or call **toll free** (855) 837-8477 (TDSTIPS), or photocopy the form below, fill it out and send it to Ted A. Moreno, 1910 Huntington Drive, Ste. 9, South Pasadena, CA 91030.

All requests will receive a reply within 48 hours to set up a time for your *Blueprint for Success Goal Setting Session.* (*Note: There will be a shipping and handling charge of $9.97 to ship the Thank You Gift Package along with the Blueprint for Success: Action Steps Guide.)

Yes Ted! I'm ready to start creating the life that I want. I want to take advantage of your FREE *Blueprint For Success Goal Setting Session,* including my personalized Actions Steps Guide and Special Thank You Gift Package.

Name_____

Address_____

City_____State_____Zip_____

Home Phone_____

Cell Phone_____

Email_____

Best time to call_____

My primary goal is: _____

_____

Made in the USA
Charleston, SC
25 October 2015